DAVE GOW

Strong Money Australia

Strong Money Australia: How to Gain Financial
Independence and Create a Life of Freedom

Contents

1

My Story and Introduction

"Your present circumstances don't determine where you can go;
they merely determine where you start." - *Nido Qubein*

"We don't want you here anymore."

Those were the words my boss said to me on a warm spring day, in the sheet metal factory where I worked.

Those words shocked me. But for some reason, I also felt calm. No stress. No panic. A wave of acceptance washed over me, and if I'm honest, even a dash of relief.

Not because I was financially independent and didn't need to work. Not even close!

Let's set the scene...

This was my first job as an adult (which I was getting fired from!).

I was renting with friends (and had bills to pay).

I had zero investments and no other income source.

So why wasn't I stressed?

Because I had one thing: savings. Enough to live on for 6-9 months. Maybe a year if I stretched it out. And this wasn't a huge pile of cash either—we're talking $20,000.

My job loss resulted in what I now call *"The Summer of Freedom."*

That summer meant the next 10 years of my life turned out very differently from the norm. I'll share that experience in a minute. But first I want to take you back to a big decision I made at age 18 and how I later lost my job.

My Big Decision

A few months after getting my license at age 18, I moved to Perth from country Victoria. Well, more specifically, a friend and I packed our bags, loaded the car with junk food, and embarked on a road trip.

We drove to Perth in my mid-90s Holden Commodore. I arrived with about $800 in the bank. We had no jobs lined up. But we had a friend's place to stay at, and Perth's economy was on fire at the time (2007), so we had zero concerns about finding work.

Why did I move? Well, I was from a small town with limited prospects. I had no job, no qualifications, and very little money. Meanwhile, some friends had recently moved to Perth and I kept hearing about the abundant jobs, the beautiful weather, and all the incredible places to see. I was sold! After all, I had nothing to lose.

Starting Work

Within a week, I found a job. The work wasn't exciting, but I was learning something and working full-time, feeling like an adult. Most of all, I was getting paid! Being unskilled factory work, the pay wasn't high – around $20/hour – but seeing that money hit the bank account each week was like Christmas.

"Wow, this is awesome!" I thought.

The work became enjoyable, and the people were good to work with. It did get extremely hot in summer though. I found it ironic that we were making air-conditioning ducts inside a sweltering hot factory. I'd jokingly call it "the sweat shop."

Despite this, I found a comfortable groove. Over the next 12 months, I even started doing some overtime. Work was busy and the extra pay was nice. My savings were building up. At that point I had no financial goals, so plenty was spent on clothes, takeaway food, and nights out drinking.

But then, something changed.

The Changing Work Environment

Our manager left. And his replacement was, well, an arsehole. He was a total dictator who wouldn't listen to reason. He made changes everybody hated. He acted like he knew better than everyone else. And with him being a large, intimidating guy, nobody dared argue with him. Morale went down. People just accepted this new reality. Everyone kept plodding along, saying nothing, and doing what they were told.

Once, the machine I was operating had some issues that needed fixing. When I made suggestions for repairing it, he said *"I don't give a shit about your opinion."*

Really? Who talks to their staff like that?

Maybe it was the shock from that moment. Maybe it was the drop in morale. But something forced me to stop and think. Why do people put up with this? Why does nobody stand up to the boss? If people were unhappy, why wouldn't they leave?

I started looking around at the other guys. But this time, I *really* looked. At their faces, demeanor, and body language. It was clear: they didn't want to be there. And now, neither did I.

At the age of 19, I was starting to see the dark side of full-time work. My future flashed before me: shuffling around this old, hot, sweaty factory in my 60s, with the same despondent look on my face. Another soulless cog in the machine. That image terrified me. *"No way in hell!"*

It became 100% clear in my mind that this future was unacceptable. No freedom and no choices...no thanks! There had to be another way. I just didn't know what it was. Yet.

At the same time, I also became curious. Why do people stay in jobs and situations they despise? It sounds naïve, but I was a teenager at the time.

So, I asked people why they stayed at this job. A few shrugged. Others said, *"I've got bills to pay."* The common vibe was this pattern of work, spend, eat, sleep, repeat, is an unavoidable reality.

The Downward Spiral

My frustrations wouldn't go away. *"I don't want to be stuck working here for the rest of my life."*

I'd now seen the dark side of full-time work. Putting up with conditions, demands, and people we don't like, in unsatisfying or meaningless jobs. All because we need money to pay bills. Why does it have to be this way?

All I could think was, *"Man, wealthy people don't have to put up with stuff like this."*

After all, if you have enough money that you don't need to work, these problems disappear. You can do whatever you like, whenever you like. I started daydreaming about what it must be like to be wealthy.

My attitude at work became worse. At first, going to work was enjoyable. Now it was a chore. I dreaded Mondays. And I resented having to work at all. My productivity collapsed. Mentally, I checked out and my care-factor declined to zero.

I'd happily roam around talking to people and take extended toilet breaks (1 hour was the record). Basically, I was milking it. Looking back, this was my way of reclaiming control and rebelling against the bullshit.

But the respect was gone. I couldn't take the workplace or my superiors seriously anymore. Without respect, the instructions and tasks are meaningless. And when things feel meaningless, your motivation disappears.

Summer was coming up and work was getting busy. Management asked us to do overtime every single day. *"I live by the beach, so I just want to hang out with my friends after work,"* I said. They didn't care and insisted on overtime. I refused.

A few unproductive weeks later, I was called into the office for a meeting. That's when I heard those fateful words: *"We don't want you here anymore."*

Management explained how I clearly didn't want to be at work. And it had reached the point where they didn't want me there either. So, we signed the paperwork and parted ways.

I said goodbye to a few people and walked out to my car, still in shock (maybe it shouldn't have been a surprise?). But driving home, I smiled, then laughed. That confused me at first. Shouldn't I be stressed out? After all, that's what people do when they lose their jobs, right? Why didn't I care?

Then it dawned on me. I wasn't worried because I had savings. I wasn't going to become homeless tomorrow. I had time to figure things out. That's when I decided: this shall be *The Summer of Freedom!* (Only I didn't have a cool name for it at the time.)

The Summer of Freedom

I spent the first few weeks of unemployment relaxing and hanging out with a mate who had just moved over from Victoria and wasn't working yet. He had some money saved from a part-time job back home.

Soon after, one of our housemates could see we were having a great time not working. So, he also quit his job! At this point, we all sound like absolute bums. But each of us were living on our own modest savings, with no government handouts.

All up, I spent about three months relaxing, going to the beach and the gym, hanging out with mates, drinking, and just enjoying the freedom. It was a simple yet profound experience. To top it off, our house was basically a run-down mansion opposite the beach, with ocean views stretching out to the horizon. The rent was $700/week, but between 4 or 5 people, that was manageable. And while this might sound like your average young adult's lazy summer, I did lots of thinking during those three months. I had multiple realisations:

- When you have savings, you have more control over your life and less stress.
- Having the freedom to control your time is priceless.
- There's no way I'm working 40 hours a week for the next 40 years.

I got a small taste of what it's like to be wealthy and independent. The freedom was intoxicating. Not having to work, while doing whatever you want, whenever you want, and still being able to pay your bills! This is what being wealthy is like? Sign me up!

At that point, I made a strong internal commitment. When I start working again, I'm going to make this dream a permanent reality. I want to build enough wealth so that I can experience this freedom all the time, forever. *I have to.* I didn't know how or when, just that I would. I couldn't become like the old guys at the factory, ground down by decades of drudgery and boredom.

The research process began, and Google became my best friend. I became obsessed with the idea of wealth and financial freedom, and spent most of my spare time reading anything I could find on the topic. Online, people said there were two main ways to create wealth: starting a business or investing.

Investing seemed easier. To me, growing and managing a business sounded stressful, complicated, and time-consuming. On the other hand, owning investments which make money passively sounded amazing.

It's true that many fortunes are made through building a successful business. In reality, however, few small businesses become big earners, and it's worth remembering that running a business is still a job, yet with more responsibility (which makes it harder to live an independent, freedom-focused lifestyle).

On the other hand, owning investments is a much more effortless way to produce wealth and passive income. And that's what creates real freedom, allowing you to spend your time doing whatever you like.

Re-joining the Workforce

Summer was over. And I now had a new goal in life: Financial Independence. While my savings were reducing, I could've kept going for another few months. But I was ready to get back to work. I wanted to start building my wealth.

My motivation came from two contrasting feelings. First: the terror of a future where I had to work forever just to exist and pay my bills. Second: the pure excitement of complete freedom and independence (where you control your time and bills are taken care of).

Fortunately, I soon found a new job which paid more than the old one. There was even afternoon and night work. After realising the generous penalty rates, working afternoons and nights became my favourite shifts. The normal rate was about $25/hour, but evening shifts took it to over $30, and Sundays paid over $50/hour! I had that Christmas-y feeling again!

At this point, all I knew was that I needed to own a portfolio of investments. To do that, I'd need to save money to buy those investments. In a very natural way, this provided more motivation to save, and less desire to spend. Side note: spenders often turn into savers once they have a meaningful and exciting *reason* to save.

With this new job began my journey to financial independence. Only I still didn't really know what to do, how to do it, or any of the things you'll read in this book.

Pursuing Freedom

As my savings built, I read books to figure out what to invest in. At the time, my online savings account was paying about 5% per annum.

I loved seeing the monthly interest hit my account. Money for nothing! My savings were earning more money each month all by themselves. How incredible! But I realised that to build wealth, I'd need to own proper investments, like shares or property, which could generate higher returns by compounding over time.

Like most Aussies, I grew up with zero understanding of the sharemarket. Squiggly lines on a chart. Green one day, red the next. Financial crises and losing 50% of your money? Pass. On the surface, it didn't look great.

Property, on the other hand, made more sense. It was familiar and easy to understand. You receive rental income and property generally increases in value over time. Plus, capital city property in Australia had performed really well for the last 50-100 years, with no large collapses.

It was settled. Property investing was going to be my path to financial freedom.

Investment Journey

Over the next couple of years, my savings grew, and I developed a decent understanding of property investing. During that time, I met my now partner and moved in with her. Being much older than me, my partner was a long-time property owner. Like most Aussies, home ownership had helped her build a modest net worth. While she wasn't bad with money, she wasn't getting anywhere either.

My ambition and focus were on display as we had 'the talk'. I explained the master plan of building enough wealth to make working optional. Luckily, she was on board and loved the idea. We didn't always see eye to eye though.

There were some tense conversations around spending, happiness, our future, and our values. (Later in this book, I'll describe how you can address similar concerns with your own partner.)

Over time, we grew to better understand each other, and found a happy middle ground. Our incomes and lifestyle were similar to our peers, yet we managed to save over 60% of our take-home pay.

At work, I'd look out the window and see a beautiful day, wishing I was free to do something else – even just sit at the park. I also couldn't shake the deep feeling that something wasn't quite right with how most of us spend our lives. At least now I knew how to escape the drudgery!

By age 23, I'd purchased two properties with my savings. That same year, my partner also purchased another property.

After our first few purchases, we joined finances and used equity in her house to buy more property. We used relatively small deposits which let us buy more assets.

These properties were in capital cities around Australia (we used buyer's agents for interstate purchases). We combined our aggressive monthly savings with equity from our properties to expand our portfolio further.

A few years later, in early 2015, we'd maxed out our borrowing capacity and I wondered how we could keep investing. That's when I took a proper look at shares, but with a slightly different approach: investing for passive income. Through this new lens, the share market started making better sense.

After doing more research, making some investments, and receiving a few dividend payments, I was convinced that shares were a good idea. We'll explore this in greater detail later in this book, along with the many things I wish I'd known when I started.

Reaching Financial Independence

After realising the simplicity and effectiveness of investing in shares for income, I had a lightbulb moment. If we put all our savings (property equity) into income-producing shares, we could actually retire soon.

In Australia, solid dividend yields and franking credits mean you can generate better passive income from shares compared to rental properties, once expenses are accounted for. We continued buying shares, our portfolio kept growing, and in late 2016, we started slowly selling our properties, with most of the proceeds going into shares and a small amount being used for our living expenses.

In 2017, we declared ourselves financially independent and promptly left work. This was around my 28th birthday.

At first, I was in shock. This dream I craved had somehow come true. As I walked out of work for the final time, my body felt electric with excitement. What would the future hold? It felt like all these new doors and possibilities had suddenly opened up for me. During the first week at home, my partner and I would look at each other and think "holy shit, we did it. We really don't have to work."

I'll share more about this transition later. But let me just say that life slowed down and got far sweeter. We began enjoying spending our time in much more varied ways, now that we didn't have to give up most of our waking lives being at work.

Things like spending more quality time together, playing with our beloved dog, and going for lots of walks. We also developed new passions. My partner threw herself into gardening, while I started a blog. I enjoyed sharing my thoughts and experiences so much that this hobby snowballed into a podcast and now a book. On top of that, we moved to a greener, more peaceful area of Perth, where we can soak in more nature, and enjoy bike rides surrounded by woodlands, wildlife, and a huge lake. We've also become involved in volunteer work like planting trees in the regional park, and helping local turtles. Even simple things like going out for lunch on a random sunny Tuesday or chilling at the beach with a coffee, just because we feel like it. The ability to do what you want, when you want, is something you can't really measure or put a price on, but it's an amazing feeling. As you can imagine, all this makes for a happier and more satisfying life than our previous full-time worker-drone situation.

It's fair to point out that my early retirement was helped along by my partner not starting from zero like I did. But in the end, this didn't make much difference, for a few reasons:

- We ended up hitting FI with more wealth than we needed.
- We could comfortably live on less than we currently spend.
- The amount of money we saved (our savings rate) roughly lines up with how long our journey took. More on this later.

After ten years in the workforce, I was ready to leave and do my own thing. If our situation was different, I would've used other strategies (contained in this book) to still create maximum freedom.

Most importantly, knowing all the stuff I'll share with you in this book, I could reach FI even faster if I started from scratch today.

That might sound absurd, but as you journey through these pages, you'll see how repeatable this goal is.

That's the thing: once you learn about financial independence and what it can do for you, *you can't unlearn it.* In the most personally empowering way, you no longer view life and money in the same way again.

Don't get me wrong, I consider myself incredibly fortunate. As you read along, you may even realise you're in a better position than you initially assumed. Regardless of where you are now, this book is a complete set of principles and lessons to help you master your financial future, with no windfalls or lucky breaks required.

Reflections on Our Journey

I learned so many lessons along the way (hence this book!). About life, finance, our mindset, and how they all intersect. Would I do things differently if I was starting over again? Absolutely.

Here's one: starting over, I wouldn't invest in property at all. Which sounds odd, because most of you reading this will be thinking, "But isn't property what helped you retire so young?"

Not really. Overall, our properties performed just okay. Some did well, yes, but others dragged it down. The real magic was our approach to household finances. Our savings rate was consistently over 60%, and even got up to 75% for a few years.

And we certainly weren't earning monster salaries. I worked as a Storeman/Forklift Driver, and my partner worked in Government Admin. While it fluctuated through the years, we earned around $75,000 each, on average (Australia's median full-time wage). This created a very healthy household income, but hardly anything out of the ordinary.

The truth is, if you save most of your pay for a number of years, and earn an okay return on your money, then it doesn't take all that long to reach the point where you have enough wealth to live on.

Importantly, we did this without sacrificing our health or happiness. The secret was cutting out the unnecessary excess that accumulated over time, like barnacles on a ship's hull. We also became good at realising what truly adds value to our lives and what is just an expensive distraction.

Yes, there is hard work involved. But consider this: ten years of hard work can create fifty years of freedom. That's an extraordinary return on your effort. Everything in this book can (and should) be tweaked to suit your own situation, your personal goals, and what you're happy with.

There are numerous stories of people all over the world doing what we've done, because they want more time, freedom, and independence than the typical full-time work arrangement gives them. I can almost guarantee that someone in a worse situation than you has achieved this. That's not to attack you, but rather to show you that this is possible. If someone who's less smart and less hard-working than you can do this, then you can too!

Now that you've heard a bit about my story, let's define what financial independence (or FIRE) is, why it's the solution to many of our problems, and why you should pursue financial independence even if you love your job.

What is FIRE?

FIRE stands for Financial Independence Retire Early. FIRE is a popular acronym, but I prefer simply 'financial independence'. That's because the 'retire early' part often creates confusion.

In simple terms, it's about building up enough investments so that you can live off these assets forever. Once the passive income you generate from investments exceeds your living expenses, you no longer need to work. You are financially independent!

This allows you to retire early if you desire. And while retirement sounds like an odd concept for someone in their 20s, 30s, or even 40s, FIRE is really about freedom and choices.

Imagine for a moment that work is completely optional. How would you live if you had complete control over your time? Would you still work the same hours in the same job? If you're like me, or most people, you'd probably say: "hell no."

And while there's numbers and finance involved, this process is more about life than it is about money. You're just solving the money side of things so you can focus more time and effort on this one special life you have.

As amazing as financial independence is, there's even more going on behind the scenes. Let's consider for a moment what most of us think of as a normal modern lifestyle.

Our Modern Lives

In Australia, and most developed countries, life runs at a frantic pace. High stress levels, anxiety, and time scarcity are accepted as a fact of life. Being 'busy' is a badge of honour. It makes us feel and sound important.

But should we be proud of this?

Across society, most of us feel like we never have enough time. We cram as much as we can manage into each day (and quite often we cram in way *more* than we can manage). We neglect our health. Our relationships deserve more time than we give them, and our hobbies wither away because we're burned out by our 'always on' culture.

Sure, we have fancier stuff than our parents did. But we're working hard to pay for it all, as each promotion or pay-rise is quickly spent on a few extra niceties...which rapidly lose their luster as we swiftly become accustomed to them.

For rare, joyful moments, we're happy. But most of the time, we're wanting to fast-forward through the present, so that we can reach the next weekend, or the next holiday. And then as soon as we reach it, we start dreading the end, when we have to return to the drudgery of work. We constantly feel like something is missing. Life seems unfulfilling. We're frustrated by our lack of freedom, and our jobs aren't meaningful. We're trapped by our expenses and our full-time schedule.

But what choice do we have?

Sure, work has its highlights. Still, most of the time we feel like a cog in a machine, and sometimes we're even treated as such. At the very least, we'd love to have more free time. We'd love to stop worrying about money.

If you're like me, you'll often stare out the window at work wondering if there's something wrong with you. Why does nobody else seem to have a problem with this? You'll have random thoughts like, *"surely there's more to life than this."* Well, there is.

Why FI Is the Solution to All of Life's Problems (Only Half Joking)

Look, financial independence won't save the world. But it does give you the power to live a more enjoyable and meaningful life. The physical, mental, and practical freedom you gain by doing things differently from the masses is astounding.

Financial independence gives you back your control. It puts you in the driver's seat with a firm grip on the steering wheel, rather than making you feel like you're being bounced around inside a pinball machine.

When you're in a strong financial position, life *is* different. Here's a taste of the many tangible benefits:

- Work is optional. Any work you do is purely because you find it enjoyable for its own sake. You can stop anytime, and the pay doesn't matter. This means we can take time to find work we truly want to do, without pressure to make a certain amount to pay the bills.
- You're no longer stressed about money. In fact, you feel good about what it can do for you, the people you love, and the world at large.
- Unlimited free time. This one is hard to imagine after so many years of work. No alarm clock necessary! Set your own schedule, or have no schedule and treat life like one big adventure. Every day feels like Saturday.
- More time with family. If you have kids (or plan to), what could be better than being fully present in their lives? You can also spend more time with pets, older family members, and friends thanks to this freedom.
- Dedicate more time to health. We no longer have to sideline this due to other demands. This is amazing (and very necessary), because without our health, what do we really have?
- We can finally spend more time on other pursuits. Those hobbies we used to have (or wish we had), the side project you yearn to explore, or

the part-time business you want to start. And the other interests we neglect because we're too tired or don't have time.

· Create the right balance in our lives. We can craft our ideal lifestyle, dedicating as much time as we want to the things that matter most. This results in a higher quality of life because we have the freedom to adjust things as our priorities change.

Why We Need Financial Independence

As you can see, financial independence has countless benefits and gives us the time and mental space to improve every area of life.

Being in a strong financial position is like playing life on easy-mode.

In fact, I'd go so far as to say we *need* Financial Independence. We need it to live healthy, balanced lives, where everything important gets the attention it deserves. There's nothing natural about working 50 hours a week for 50 years. Instead of having no time for anything, you'll have time for everything.

Would you do your current job for free? Probably not. So it's fair to say that you'd rather do other things with your time. I know it can be hard to imagine what else to do, given we're so accustomed to our current way of life. But that's exactly why you need FI, so you can figure out who you are and what really matters to you.

That might sound a bit strange, so let me explain. The rat race dulls our imagination, our spirit, and our sense of who we are. But once you escape from its tentacles, you reclaim your soul. I'm not saying you won't work anymore. You probably will. Except this time it will probably feel more like 'play' than 'work.' Almost everybody who reaches FI still works in some form. But their energy and focus shifts to what's meaningful to them.

Sometimes it's being the best damn parent they can be. Other times it's starting a business that can make a difference and help a lot of people. Or they might decide to explore multiple things each week: fitness, hobbies, volunteering for important causes, and more.

In many cases, people are just happy to experience a cruisier lifestyle. For example, working 2 or 3 days per week gives them time and space to focus on other stuff, achieving a healthy sense of balance. Instead of making life fit around work, work can fit around life.

Of course, there's no one-size-fits-all recipe. That's the beauty of it. Financial independence lets you create the ideal life *for you.*

Take a moment to imagine what you might like to do if you didn't have to work. Think about your life 5, 10, 15 years from now. What kind of future do you want for yourself? What would your ideal day look like? Write it down, and then once you're feeling excited about it, realise that this doesn't have to be some pointless daydream: it can become a reality, and this book will show you how.

Why Should You Pursue FI Even If You Love Your Job

Some people seek Financial Independence because they want to escape unsatisfying work or a high-pressure career. Others are motivated by the desire for a simpler life, spending time how they please, and the flexibility to scale work up and down as it suits them. Another (rarer) group loves their work and the idea of retiring early is madness.

"Why would you not just do something you love? Why would you want to leave the workforce? I love my job and can't imagine doing anything else!"

If this is you, congratulations! Seriously. But understand, you're very much in the minority. Most of us end up in relatively uninspiring work because we need the money. Sometimes we aren't sure what our passions are, and we don't have spare time to figure it out. Even if we do know, it's not always easy to match our interests, current skills, and employment opportunities.

If you are in this group of what I'll call 'the happy workers', you've hit the jackpot.

But here's why you should still work towards Financial Independence:

- You love your job now, but that can change. A new boss could change the morale and workplace dynamic very quickly. Soon, an enjoyable job could become something you dread due to factors outside your control. You may also lose passion for the industry as things become stale, or evolve in ways you don't like.
- You could lose your job and find it hard to get a new one. Depending on your industry, your employer may downsize staff levels, outsource more work, or use more automation and software. Being in a strong financial position protects you against this risk. Plus, strong finances gives you plenty of time to search for a new job, rather than feeling pressured to quickly get back in the workforce after becoming unemployed.
- If you continue to spend all your current income, you're extremely vulnerable to economic shocks or reductions in earnings. This creates a level of background anxiety and stress whether you realise it or not. Your situation is less certain than you think.
- If you have children, or a family member gets sick, your priorities might change. That job may be great, but you'd give anything to spend more time elsewhere. As you build savings and investments, your ability to re-allocate your time increases. You gain more control over your life and can change course at any moment.
- The practical and psychological benefits of having rock-solid finances means you can move through life with the confidence that you can deal with just about anything. You have the power to deal with challenges without much stress. You become a more resilient human being.
- Work is more enjoyable when you don't need the money. You're not afraid of losing your job, which ironically, makes you better at it. You can speak out against corporate nonsense, give your honest thoughts, and even say no to certain tasks which your co-workers might feel pressured into due to their slavish reliance on a pay check.

The most common feedback I hear from readers of my blog and others in the FIRE community (even if they're only 12 months into their journey) is how much more relaxed and confident they feel about life.

Knowing you have savings and investments gives you an invisible coat of armour. So, now that you're thoroughly convinced that pursuing FI is the best thing since sliced bread, here's what you can expect to learn in this book.

What You'll Learn

- How and why this great opportunity for freedom has been created.
- The fundamentals of FIRE and how to tailor it to your personal situation.
- Why freedom and independence is the best thing you can buy.
- My most important lessons on personal finance and building wealth.
- How to live a great life while increasing your savings rate.
- Which investments are best for retiring early and building passive income.
- How to increase your income and make more money.
- How to start investing and build a portfolio, even if you're a total investing rookie.
- Strategies to optimise your mortgage and superannuation.
- Timeless investment principles to ensure long term success.
- How to adjust course and stay motivated when life gets in the way.
- How to plan for and transition into your ideal life.

Okay, so I've made a few promises there. You might be sceptical. Why am I the right person to write this book?

Why This Book Is Worth Reading

Look, I know there are thousands of finance books out there. Many are written by extremely smart people. But let me tell you why this one is worth reading.

I explain things simply and clearly, so you can understand even if you have no finance background or didn't finish school (like me).

I'm completely self-taught, so I've learned valuable lessons about what to do (and what not to do) to become financially independent at a young age.

I'm not pushing any crazy investment ideas or gimmicks. Nor will I try to sell you any courses or coaching to learn more 'secrets' at the end of this book. All my 'secrets' are in these pages.

My focus is purely on financial independence and creating freedom as quickly as possible. This isn't generic advice to help you build wealth for old age.

This book is 100% tailored to Australians: our incomes and living costs, tax system, superannuation, and investment options.

I've been in your shoes before, so I know what it's like to have a desire for wealth and freedom and not know exactly how to get there.

What to Expect

You'll learn how to invest effectively and become very wealthy over time, but this book is not a get rich quick scheme.

It has all the important information you need to change your finances and create the life you want, done with sensible long-term income-producing investments. But it does require effort and action to achieve results.

There's also no bullshit or hype. Just practical strategies for reaching financial independence in Australia. You'll learn everything I wish I knew back when I was blindly searching for how to retire early. And, finally, you can expect my honest guidance, simple and actionable steps, and nuggets of wisdom to help you clarify the best path forward on your journey.

You may still have some reservations. Maybe I'm a freak outlier case which can't be repeated. Maybe you feel this won't work for you. Or maybe you think "if this is real, why doesn't everyone do it?"

And I'll admit being financially independent and retired by 30 sounds ridiculous. So, in the next chapter, I'll address these concerns. Is this *really* possible? And if FI *is* achievable, why are we only hearing about it in recent years? More importantly, is this repeatable for lots of people, or just a lucky few?

2

Our Opportunity for Freedom

"A pessimist sees the difficulty in every opportunity; an optimist sees the opportunity in every difficulty." - *Winston Churchill*

We have an incredible opportunity for freedom that is overlooked by almost everyone in society. In fact, most people would scoff at the idea. But in this chapter, I'll explain how financial independence is possible for almost everyone in Australia, even if they don't realise it. You may have already decided that being FI sounds pretty sweet. So let me show you that, not only is it possible, but that it's a realistic and achievable goal for middle class Aussies to shoot for. And, more importantly, you can experience this luxurious freedom while you're young and healthy and energetic enough to make the most of it. Sure, being financially secure in your 60s is nice. But it's way better to be able to do whatever you want, whenever you want, from your 30s and beyond. What are those 30 extra years of freedom worth to you?

And not to be morbid, but what if we only live to 70? Or 55? Sometimes people pin all their plans and dreams on a beautiful retirement at 65, for just a few short years of enjoyment. Or, sadder still, they might leave this Earth even sooner than they expected. Retiring early gives us the time and space to really experience and appreciate our lives for as long as we're lucky enough to be here.

In this chapter, you'll learn how this incredible opportunity for freedom has come about due to changes in the global economy. You'll see how our incomes and wealth have developed over time.

I'll also show you how the cost of living has changed and how that feeds into this whole dynamic. Lastly, we'll tie it off with some important takes on consumption, happiness, and how advertising hacks our psychology to steal our money.

When we understand how we got to where we are today, we develop a greater perspective. This gives us a birds-eye view of the world, and shows us the way forward.

Okay, let's get started!

The Global Economy: A Wealth Generating Machine

For most of human history, our standard of living was roughly the same. We simply lived off the land, hunting and foraging. If we had a safe place to sleep and enough food to eat, life was good.

But over time, things changed.

Modern societies developed and we started trading with each other. Capitalism was embraced, and factories popped up as mass production took off. The pace of progress and advancements in tools and technology started speeding up.

GDP per capita, 1820 to 2018

This data is adjusted for differences in the cost of living between countries, and for inflation. It is measured in constant 2011 international-$.

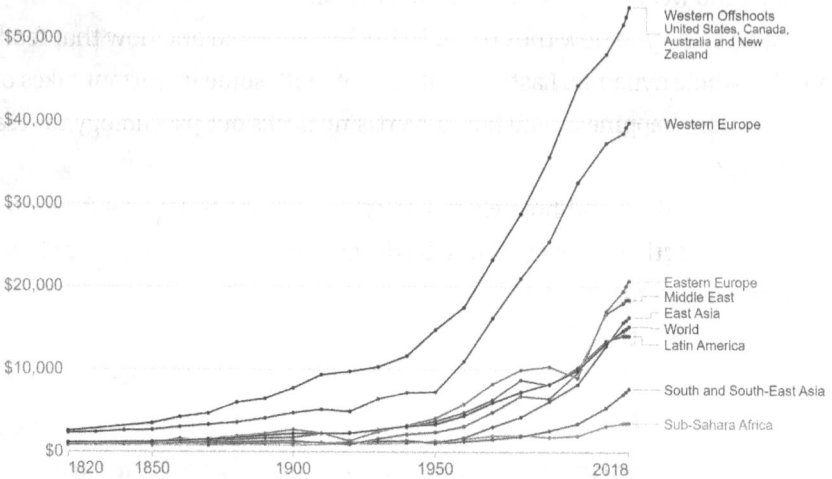

```
$50,000                                                    Western Offshoots
                                                           United States, Canada,
                                                           Australia and New
                                                           Zealand

$40,000                                                    Western Europe

$30,000

$20,000                                                    Eastern Europe
                                                           Middle East
                                                           East Asia
                                                           World
                                                           Latin America
$10,000
                                                           South and South-East Asia

                                                           Sub-Sahara Africa
$0
      1820    1850        1900        1950        2018
```

Source: Maddison Project Database 2020 (Bolt and van Zanden, 2020)   OurWorldInData.org/economic-growth • CC BY

In the last 100 years alone, there has been a huge explosion in prosperity across many countries, with Western economies like Australia being the biggest winners. Our living standards have been climbing for a long time.

We see this every day. Insanely powerful supercomputers in our pocket. The ultra-safe and comfortable cars we drive. The fact that we can afford international travel, near-limitless restaurant food, regular beauty treatments, new kitchens, and so on. What is commonplace today would have been unthinkable even for the most powerful people in the world 200 years ago.

We barely think twice about this stuff for two reasons:

1. Small, consistent improvements are hard to notice until you step back and zoom out.
2. These things are normalised, so we take them for granted.

But it wasn't always this way. If you doubt this for a second, ask anyone over 50 how much things have changed during their lifetime.

Capitalism, despite its issues, has played a pivotal role in this outcome. Our semi-regulated, mostly free-enterprise system has brought many wonderful innovations and created massive wealth, employment, and increasing luxury.

How Has This Happened?

Humans have an irresistible urge to make progress and improve their lives, and capitalism incentivises this. Capitalism motivates us to create new things, solve problems, and do more with less, because if we can provide value to others, we're financially rewarded. Of course, there's more to life than money, and non-paid work is incredibly important (if not more so). But for now, we're talking about the economic system as it relates to income, wealth, and financial independence, and this incentive system is the backbone behind humanity's progress.

Ongoing investment into new projects, machinery, and technology creates great innovations and efficiencies, resulting in more output per person over time. Each little improvement makes us more productive. This allows companies to earn more profit from the same amount of customers. Yet, customers also increase over time due to population growth and rising living standards. In turn, companies can pay higher wages while creating wealth for shareholders.

The key here is productivity and efficiency. Every incremental improvement creates higher profits and/or lower costs. This value-creation process has meant we enjoy higher incomes than before (even after adjusting for inflation). The global economic machine isn't perfect, but it's delivered increased affluence and prosperity for so many people, and will continue to do so.

Let's take a closer look at how our lives have changed.

A Brief History of Household Spending

An eye-opening study into household spending from 1900 to 2000 was compiled using data from the United States Bureau of Labor Statistics. Given how similar our lifestyles are, we can safely assume that Australia followed similar trends.

Back in 1900, almost half the country worked in agriculture, with many people living on the farms where they worked. On average, citizens spent 80% of their income on food, clothing, and housing costs. Few people owned a home. Only a fraction had gas or electricity, let alone flushing toilets.

Only rich people owned a car, and even then, it looked like a fancy golf cart. Nobody had a smartphone (I know, crazy), and only 5% of people had a home telephone. There were no TVs, no streaming services, and you can be pretty confident the weekly food budget didn't include UberEats or brunch at the local cafe.

Here's where their money went:

Category	% Of Household Spending
Food	43%
Housing	23%
Clothing	14%
Healthcare	5%
Entertainment	2%
Other	13%

Again, these people lived an unthinkably basic lifestyle. You might find it hard to relate to them. But here's the crazy thing: this was only a few generations ago. Perhaps even your Mum's or Dad's grandparents.

Fast Forward to 1950

With improving technology, many industries became more productive. This had the double benefit of lowering costs and increasing profits. Thanks to increasing wages, people could afford to buy more goods and services.

Nicer clothes, new home appliances, maybe a television. Car ownership became more common. In 1950, only around 10% of the population worked in farming, with many now working in factories. Household spending started to change.

Category	% Of Household Spending
Food	30%
Housing	28%
Clothing	12%
Healthcare	5%
Entertainment	4%
Other	21%

The biggest difference here is the fall in food costs relative to wages, now consuming 30% of income compared to 43% before. The 'other' category has also grown, in line with increasing prosperity and living standards. Overall, life got a bit fancier and more convenient.

End of Study in 2003

Technology and computing power continued its relentless progress, combined with international trade, leading to greater efficiencies and purchasing power. Let's take another look at household spending. Get ready for a shock...

Category	% Of Household Spending
Food	13%
Housing	33%
Clothing	4%
Healthcare	6%
Entertainment	5%
Other	39%

Holy moly! Food and clothing costs have plummeted. In 1900, these two categories formed 57% of household spending. Now they're just 17%.

Interestingly, about 40% of incomes are now being directed to the 'other' category. Where is this money going? We'll get to that soon. But for now, it's safe to say that much of this category is extra stuff we've added to our lives over time because we could afford to. Our ancestors would barely recognise our current lives.

Now, let's put it all together to see the changes since 1900:

	1900	1950	2003
Food	43%	30%	13%
Housing	23%	28%	33%
Clothing	14%	12%	4%
Healthcare	5%	5%	6%

In the 20 years since the end of this study, the same trend of increasing living standards has continued. But that's America, famous for its wealth and excess. How about little old Australia?

Let's check how the average Aussie's income has changed over time. And then, so we've got a clear picture, we'll compare that to changes in the cost of living. Because if the price of stuff is going up at the same rate as our incomes, then we're no better off, are we?

How Inflation Affects Purchasing Power

Most of us understand how inflation works. For example, a loaf of bread costs 10 times more than it did in 1975. We're used to seeing this happen over time. And with many things, not just bread.

But what about the stuff that falls in price? Or, more commonly, what about when things increase in price, but at a *slower* rate than our incomes? When this happens, we can buy *more* products and services with the same portion of our income. Put another way, *our purchasing power has increased.*

Let's say the cost of living – also known as CPI (Consumer Price Index) – is increasing at 2% per year. And let's say wages are growing by 3% per year. Life has become more expensive, but our earnings went up slightly faster. Despite rising costs, we have more real income than before.

When this occurs, we can save more, spend more, or do whatever we want with the extra cash. And the good news? This is exactly what's happened for the last 100+ years. It's evident from the US study I just mentioned, and in our living standards, too: there's so many things we can now afford that we couldn't before.

Now, to make this more concrete, let's see how incomes in Australia have fared against inflation.

Income versus Inflation

According to the Australian Bureau of Statistics (ABS), in 1966 the average full-time worker earned around $60 per week.

In 2016, the average full-time worker was earning $1,516 per week, or $78,832 per year. This means wages grew at around 6.7% per annum over that 50-year span. According to the Reserve Bank of Australia (RBA), the average annual inflation rate over those 50 years was 5.2%.

The result? Real wages grew by 1.5% per year.

"Wow, 1.5% per year," you say, rolling your eyes. Big deal, right?

Well, because of compounding, this is a big deal. If wage growth matched inflation (5.2% per annum), an income of $60 per week in 1966 would be $758 per week in 2016. But full-time wages were **double that!**

Here's a simple graph to show what happened in the last 50 years.

Australian Full-time Wage vs Inflation

— Wages — Inflation

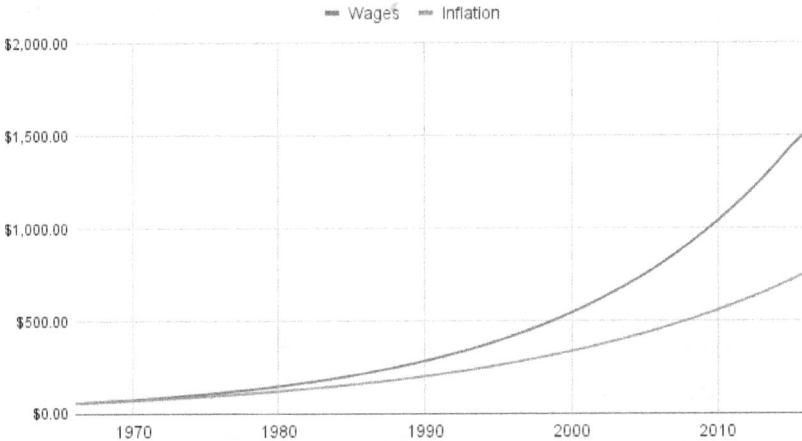

Even if we make a ridiculous assumption that 1966 wages were only *just enough to survive*, with absolutely nothing leftover, this means we still have *twice as much income now* after adjusting for inflation.

This is not unusual. The same slow and steady trend has continued since then, and it played out during the previous 50 years as well. In fact, real wages in Australia are almost 400% higher than they were in 1900.

This is why some people can save huge amounts of their pay without dumpster diving for food or living in a cardboard box. And it's why financial independence is now a realistic option.

Now, some people assume the income figures are skewed upwards by rich people with huge earnings. But that's untrue. Here's why: By 2021, the average full-time wage had increased to $1,737 per week, or $90,324 per year. The *median* full-time wage grew to a healthy $1,499 per week, or $77,948 per year.

Being the median, this is the middle point. So, half the full-time workers earn more than this, and half earn less. And to be clear, this does not include bonuses or overtime, which are common in many jobs.

However you slice it, full-time incomes have doubled in the last 50-odd years after inflation. So, we should be able to save half our pay without too much trouble, right? But that's not what happened, which begs the question: where the hell has the money gone?

At this point, some people start getting flustered. We're accustomed to hearing how hard we've got it, not how much better things have become. Out comes the granddaddy of excuses...

"Those inflation numbers must be wrong!"

To understand changes in the economy and the financial prosperity of Australians, the RBA tracks the cost of living over time. To do this, they create a 'basket' of goods and services which is designed to represent the cost of an average Aussie lifestyle. So, when you hear, "figures from the Reserve Bank show the cost of living/inflation rose by 3% for the year", that's where it comes from.

If you ask a typical Aussie, they'd say inflation is higher than what is reported. That's because our minds (and the media) tend to focus intensely on stuff which gets more expensive, while ignoring things that become cheaper. But according to an RBA research paper, the inflation figures typically **overstate** what a household experiences:

- As the price of goods and services change, it's assumed that our behaviour stays the same. But when we tweak our spending as prices change, by shopping around or substituting items, we experience lower inflation than is assumed.
- The CPI figures ignore online shopping options and the absolute bonanza of lower cost products available to us, compared to what's available in traditional stores.
- The basket of goods and services is adjusted every few years to become more 'relevant'. As households adopt newer products, additional services, and fancier stuff, it's included in the tracked prices. This overstates the underlying cost of living.

· The basket doesn't properly adjust for quality. On average, goods and services improve in quality over time. A modern TV is a lot different from one 20 years ago.

So, the inflation figures are quite generous. In essence, it doesn't even track the cost of the same things over time. Instead, it's measuring the cost of increasingly fancier things and completely optional luxuries which are added to our lives. Yet despite this, our incomes have *still* outstripped these costs over time.

The reason we don't feel flush with cash is because we've ratcheted up our spending. The truth is, we've become consumption machines. Our desires and tastes keep expanding to match our income. This ensures we always feel stuck, like we're just trying to keep our head above water. Our 'wants' have increased at the same rate as our spending capacity (often more).

Consumption Machines

Here's the RBA's take on this phenomenon:

"Over time, individuals may not compare the cost of achieving the same standard of living, but rather that of a 'reasonable' standard of living. Real consumption per person has risen substantially over time, indicating that living standards have increased.

"What is a reasonable standard of living has also increased, as households have become accustomed to consuming more goods and services and those of a higher quality. As a result, perceived increases in the cost of living may partly reflect the cost of attaining a higher standard of living for many households.

"There is also evidence that individuals' perceptions about their wellbeing are formed not purely in absolute terms, but partly by comparing themselves with those around them – colloquially termed 'keeping up with the Joneses'"

Real Household Consumption per Capita
March quarter 1990 = 100

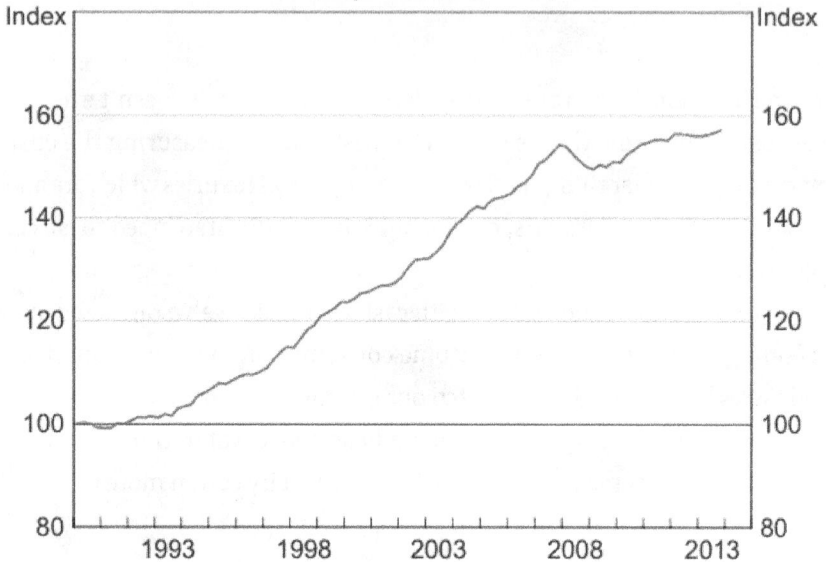

Sources: ABS; RBA

Another humorous way to highlight this is to consider Parkinson's Law, which states that work expands to fill the time available for its completion. Basically, the amount of time you have available is how long it takes to complete a task.

In our personal finances, spending expands to consume all available income. However much we earn, we seem to allocate every single dollar (and more, thanks to debt) to dozens of little 'lifestyle upgrades'. Basically, it burns a hole in our pocket!

And while we might laugh at the absurdity of this behaviour, these high consumption lifestyles aren't great for the world at large. As a society, we're becoming increasingly aware just how much our over-consumption habits can cause ugly, destructive side effects.

Australians are consistently ranked among the richest citizens in the world on a per-person basis. We are regularly in the top 3 countries when it comes to personal wealth. Yet the average Aussie would probably dismiss the previous charts and angrily tell you where to shove them! That's because the media is constantly pandering to our victim mentality, telling us how terrible things are. For others, they become trapped playing an unwinnable 'comparison game', focusing on what others have that they don't.

Today, the greatest benefits come to those who try to save some of this increased income. We can benefit twice over by investing our savings into productive companies. This then takes on a life of its own, creating wealth and another source of increasing income over time.

"But what about debt? Don't we have higher debt these days?"

Yes, we do. But debt doesn't diminish the expanding wealth and income we've experienced. By the way, we'll discuss debt and housing (as that's what the debt is usually for!) later in this book.

The truth is, debt levels have increased because, like everything else, we can afford more of it. People have chosen to borrow because it's affordable. If it wasn't, we simply couldn't service the debt. But for the most part, we very much can.

Think of it like a weighing scale. Over the last 50 years, incomes have grown and interest rates have reduced. This lightens the scale. So, people have chosen to add more debt, which weighs down the scale while still keeping it 'balanced'.

Debt is also a choice. You can avoid debt your entire life and still get the economic benefits of increasing real income and investment returns.

A Caveat

Look, I'm not saying everything is sunshine and rainbows and that our economic machine works great for everyone. There are always exceptions and life is genuinely rough for some people. So, I'm able to say this from a position of good fortune and privilege.

Building wealth and financial independence will always prove unattainable for a certain portion of the population. Sadly, many Aussies live week-to-week, with their earnings going out as fast as it comes in. We saw this during the coronavirus, with newly jobless people unable to pay next week's rent or buy food for their family.

Now, some people have genuinely tough life circumstances. But when middle-class Australians live week-to-week, this is usually the result of poor financial habits. That might be painful to accept. But the broader picture tells us that improving our financial position is easier than ever before. And it starts by dealing with the nonsense of consumerism.

Consumerism

I've noticed a disturbing trend in recent years. Despite our increasing standard of living, many Aussies grow more unsatisfied each year. This discontent is driven by ever-expanding desires, and the belief that if we can satisfy them, life will finally be good. The void will be filled.

Consumerism has blossomed into a religion in the last 50 years, fuelled by our increasing incomes. The fundamental premise? Buy more stuff = better life = happiness. This philosophy was gobbled up like a big ol' bag of chocolate chip cookies. It tasted great at first, but people became hooked on the sugar-high of 'more stuff'. And now it's making us sick.

Case in point: we've run out of room in our homes to store our increasing possessions, and a growing industry of self-storage facilities has boomed.

Even though the average Aussie home is bigger than ever, we still can't fit all our crap inside!

Luckily, many of us now see consumerism as bad for the planet, bad for our finances, and bad for our mental health. Problem solved, right? Well, not so fast. Like a virus, consumerism has cleverly redesigned itself.

Consumerism 2.0: Novelty and marketing

At this stage, our desire for more stuff has been met many times over. And at the same time, society's wealth continues to grow.

How do you convince people to part with their cash when they're already overflowing with stuff? Convince them that they need *better stuff*. Higher quality. More luxurious. More features. A richer experience. They've even created a term for it. Mass-tige: prestige for the masses.

Genius, right? And it's working. *We've swapped the pursuit of more, for the pursuit of better.*

Home developers, fashion designers, product creators, car manufacturers, travel operators. All are pushing higher options to the masses. And the implied payoff for the consumer is the same: status, envy, luxury, approval from others, and the appearance that you're winning at life.

Not because we need it, of course. At this point, we don't need a damn thing. It's just another bag of cookies with a different flavour. But these are even more addictive, because unlike the 'more stuff' cookies, the 'better stuff' cookies are a bottomless packet.

There is a limit to how much stuff we can own. But there is no limit to better.

We keep munching away, thinking we're getting somewhere, while the cookies are replenished faster than we can eat them. So we chew faster, trying to take it all in. Better technology, holidays, cars, clothes, and restaurants. A life of never-ending upgrades.

Many of us are addicted to this cycle of *better*. We're addicted to newness.

We're still trying to buy happiness, and we compensate for our lack of free time with more short-term treats. But it's not working. Do people look happier to you? No, me neither. If anything, people seem more anxious and less satisfied than ever.

The sugar-high from spending money makes us feel wealthy in the short term, but leaves us close to broke in the long term.

The Truth about Marketing

The advertising industry should really be called the manipulation industry. The goal? To make us feel like we *need* whatever they're selling. To feel more successful, more attractive, and gain greater status and respect from our peers and the world. We aren't buying products, we're buying feelings. But the truth is, we can get all our happy, positive vibes in better ways than handing over all our cash.

Clever marketers are working relentlessly to hijack our emotions and manipulate us into buying things. They even create desires where none existed before. Every word, every camera shot, every angle, even the music, is carefully crafted to make us feel a certain way.

Back in the old days, ads used to show a product, and someone would explain the item. Consumers could then make a rational choice about whether to buy based on the information provided.

But then savvy marketers realised they could play on our emotions. For example, smoking was literally advertised to women as 'torches of freedom', as it was one of the few things a woman could do to assert her independence 100 years ago. It was marketed as glamorous and brave. And (sadly for women's health) it worked.

There are countless examples like this. Once we sit back and look at most advertising objectively, we can see how silly it all is. And that gives us incredible power. I like to call this: *developing a bullshit detector*.

Here are some mental tips to hone your bullshit detector and beat the marketers at their silly manipulation game:

- Ignore advertising of any kind. You can install free extensions on your computer to block ads from showing on the internet, which helps.
- Never buy on impulse. Delay the purchase to make sure you really want it.
- Consider if your mood is affecting your thinking (we often buy things if we're feeling down, or tired, or hungry).
- Would you still make this purchase if you couldn't show or tell anyone else?
- Do you need this, or is it just a fancier version of what you already have?
- Can you achieve the same feelings or desired result in a better or lower cost way?
- Is this removing genuine pain? Or is it promising a new source of pleasure? For example: maybe you have a smoothie blender that only works well half the time. If you use it every day, it could make sense to replace it. But if you're thinking about buying a drone, you're probably not suffering pain from the lack of a drone, so the pleasure it gives you might be short-lived.

Without these filters, you'll be easily led into all sorts of unplanned purchasing decisions. But with a finely tuned bullshit detector, you become a much more powerful and self-aware human.

In terms of personal finance, this creates a massive gap between thoughtless consumers and conscious spenders. As the world becomes wealthier, this trend will continue. Make thoughtful financial choices and you'll be handsomely rewarded with lower stress, higher levels of saving, more contentment, and the ability to live a life of your own choosing decades earlier than your peers.

Everyone else will simply repeat the work/spend hamster wheel and wonder why they're getting nowhere. You, on the other hand, will see consumerism and marketing for the bubbling-over cauldron of bullshit that it really is. And then you'll probably find it hilarious.

You're now an independent thinker, and part of the financial independence community. Our job is to cut through the garbage marketed at us from every direction. We must sit back and think critically about purchases. Do we really need this thing? How quickly will the sugar-high wear off? And will this make me any happier over the long term?

Get excited about being a selective spender. This is the main tool in creating genuine wealth and freedom, because you're not saving up money to never spend. Instead, you're going to spend that money on the greatest purchase of all: buying your freedom, one bit at a time.

Side note: being content with what we have makes our lives happier right now. Rather than endlessly chasing new versions of the same thing. It allows us to slow down and feel more grateful. It frees us from the urge to compete and keep up with the novelty chasers.

Many people right now are chasing bigger, fancier versions of what they already have. This is a perpetual loop to nowhere. Financial independence, and happiness itself, is built on the opposite side of the scale. In contentment. In simplicity. And in the things we *don't* need. This allows us to effortlessly save and invest plenty of our income, until we gain true control over our lives, forever.

But What about the Good Life?

Before we get carried away, there are hurdles. That's right! What, did you think you'd be retired by next week? Don't worry, these hurdles are mostly solved with mindset shifts. Like this one: there's a faulty assumption that you have to miss out on 'the good life' to save more. This is false.

We're blinded by living in an era of bingeing, excess, and extremism. I'm not suggesting you become a monk and abstain from all your desires (though I can think of worse things, as monks are seemingly very happy!). But the fact is, those who can manage even a moderate level of self-control and balance – whether through willpower, habits or lifestyle design – have an enormous advantage. This simple principle is called *The Art of Moderation*.

The Lost Art of Moderation

Moderation means enjoying something in a sensible amount. Not too much, not too little. Importantly, there is a healthy level of limitation built into this enjoyment.

Why does moderation matter? It helps us avoid terrible outcomes from indulging in excess like a wealthy Roman Emperor. Whether that's alcohol, food, work, entertainment, sex, or other things humans are prone to do in extreme quantities.

Constantly trying to satisfy our short-term cravings is an unhealthy and self-destructive way to live, because our brains aren't wired to be satisfied. They aren't wired to say, "okay, I'm good now." They're wired to say, "I want more."

The reason for this is biological. Striving for more is a built-in survival instinct. Early humans who accumulated more resources and hunted more food had a higher chance of living and reproducing. Not much has changed today. But we no longer live in scarcity. We live in abundance, with unlimited access to food and other pleasures which our brains struggle to handle.

Most of us realise that 'toning it down' is generally good. By avoiding excess, we get better physical and mental health, higher levels of life satisfaction, and the quiet confidence of knowing we're in control.

Put another way, we can benefit from our caveperson instinct to strive and build wealth, and also reap the rewards of a modern-day human. We get to put forth effort in accumulating resources, and then enjoy greater peace and happiness, knowing we're safe to enjoy our freedom and abundance without fearing for survival.

Moderation works the same way when it comes to money. We don't need to avoid things that cost money. Rather, we enjoy the benefits of modern life in sensible quantities – in moderation – which makes a massive difference to our finances. This works because of a strange quirk known as *Hedonic Adaptation*.

Hedonic Adaptation

Hedonic adaptation is the tendency for humans to adapt to new life circumstances relatively quickly and return to our 'baseline' level of happiness.

One well-known example is the happiness levels of lottery winners compared to recent paraplegics. After about 12-24 months, both returned to their baseline happiness levels. Basically, the lottery winner discovered life wasn't as great as she expected. And the paraplegic found that life wasn't as terrible as he expected.

We can notice this in our own lives, too. Consider the experience of moving into a new house, getting a pay rise, or buying a new phone. After an initial burst of excitement and pleasure, we quickly adapt to the situation and it becomes normal. The result? We feel much the same as before.

This quirk plays out in our personal finances. As our income grows, we tend to increase our spending. Yet we don't understand why we're not getting ahead, and soon the thought of a reduced income or spending less feels scary. We've adapted to our new situation, yet we're no happier. It's simply become our new normal. It's no coincidence that our work-spend lifestyles are like a treadmill. We're running, but staying in the same spot.

One way to counter this is to automatically increase your savings the instant your pay goes up. And I mean the *instant* you get that rise. Say you get a $10,000 pay rise: before that extra pay comes in, set up a system to automatically put that increased money towards your savings. In other words, pretend the pay rise never happened. Don't let yourself adjust to having more money. This helps you avoid the dreaded 'lifestyle inflation', where your expenses magically grow to meet your income.

Of course, if you make efforts to increase your income (there's strategies in chapter seven) you're allowed to increase your spending. As long as most of your extra pay is directed towards savings, you're still better off.

There's another big lesson here: we can make lifestyle changes and create new spending habits that help us become financially independent with no reduction in happiness.

The best part about habits is that they're effortless. With each repetition, our financial decisions become a self-reinforcing loop, effortlessly pushing us towards our goals.

Even if we perceive those changes as negative at first, we'll soon wonder what the fuss was about. Our ability to adapt and thrive is far greater than we give ourselves credit for.

But hedonic adaptation also tells us something else. Financial Independence won't magically *make us* happy by itself. Nothing amazing happens when we reach FI (apart from not having to work, which I guess is kind of amazing!). Yes, FI gives us the space and time to create a happier life, by letting us focus our time and energy on what's most important, without bills and job commitments getting in the way. But it's still up to us to build a meaningful life.

Hack Your Happiness

The reason this works is because there is no magic level of spending which creates a good life. You can hold some arbitrary number in your mind, like $50,000 per year, or $200,000, but it's completely made up.

We adapt to new conditions, whether we think they're good or bad. The secret to a good life starts with our mindset, the way we meet our needs, and how we approach each day. This is all rooted in our habits and our outlook.

You can have a great day spending $5,000...or $0. One is not necessarily better. Both options are a choice. We can chase an expensive lifestyle if we want, but there's always a trade-off, and we'll sacrifice more in pursuit of it. And, in all likelihood, when we get there and the novelty wears off, we'll realise we don't actually feel that different.

Modern life is already incredible. Pushing it to the extreme is not going to give us permanently elevated happiness. In fact, the opposite is probably true.

The more things you can appreciate, the richer your life is. The multi-millionaire who refuses to be grateful will have a miserable experience compared to a moderately well-off Aussie who appreciates each day and keeps in mind all the things they are thankful for.

During the last 100 years, there have been many people who amassed enough wealth to retire from business or work to focus on other things. But today, more and more middle-class people are realising it's possible to save, invest, and retire *far earlier* than the standard 65-70 years of age.

Takeaways

In this chapter, we learned...

- How the global economy has become more productive, leading to higher wealth.
- That the portion of our income needed to pay for genuine essentials has shrunk.
- How Australian wages have doubled in the last 50 years, even after inflation.
- Our lifestyles are dramatically different from previous generations, with more conveniences and luxuries than our ancestors could ever imagine.
- How we've become used to spending more, buying newer things, and chasing experiences.
- How advertising convinces us to buy things we don't need.
- How we're trying to purchase happiness to create meaning and compensate for our lack of freedom. But it's not working.

Yes, the world has problems. There are *always* problems. But the truth is, we have more wealth and income than ever before in history. Yet, despite that, our current lifestyles are stressful and unsatisfying. Instead of chasing short-term highs that don't make us happier, we should save and invest to buy our freedom.

Hopefully, you're beginning to see the massive opportunity in front of you, and the problem with our current work-spend hamster-wheel lifestyles. You want to join the people taking control of their finances and creating freedom in their lives.

So where do we start? First, we'll discuss the fundamentals of financial independence and how this works.

3

The Fundamentals of Financial Independence

"The price of anything is the amount of life you give in exchange for it." - *Henry David Theroux*

On one hand, financial independence is exciting and life-changing. Yet it's also incredibly simple, even boring. FI lets you choose how to spend every waking hour of your day. That's exciting! However, to achieve this, all you have to do is save and invest for a decent period of time. Boring.

Basically, we take a good chunk of our income and put it into sensible long-term investments. (Don't worry, these investments are easy to understand, hassle-free, and you can start with very little cash.)

Over time, those investments grow. Eventually, they become large enough to pay for our lifestyle forever. So, how much do you need to invest to be financially independent? That's exactly what we'll discuss in this chapter. Along with...

- Savings rates and how long it takes to retire early.
- Tweaking your goal to suit your desired lifestyle.
- How to semi-retire and bring your freedom forward.

- The importance of our values and philosophy.
- Building a happy life without spending all our money.

Sounds good? Let's get started.

How Much Do You Need to Be FI?

First, you need to know how much your investments can reliably generate for you each year. This will reveal how much you'll need to save to reach your goal.

Side note: even after all this time, investing still amazes me. The idea that you can use your money to earn more money, forever, is incredible. I don't think I'll ever get over it.

If you're investing in the share market (which I would suggest), it can be tricky to figure out a reliable return figure. After all, shares – like most investments – don't always produce the same returns every year.

Our best bet is to make an educated estimate and apply common sense.

Let's look at the history of share market returns. According to Credit Suisse, since 1900 the world average for share market returns has been 5.2% per year, after inflation. This is the total return (dividend income and capital growth) minus inflation.

This average includes countries which did poorly, and countries which did great. Interesting fact: since 1900, Australia has been one of the best performing share markets, returning about 6.5% after inflation (or 10% total return before inflation).

So, let's say our investments will provide long-term returns of 7-8% per year in dividends and capital growth, or 5% per year after inflation. This means we could live off 4% of our portfolio, increase our spending with inflation, and never run out of money. The reason we need to account for inflation is to ensure our investment income can rise over time to pay our bills well into the future as the cost of living rises.

But in practice, there's more to it than that. The share market is a volatile beast, with very strong years, and unfortunately, some painful years. How do we account for that? Luckily, this has been studied extensively by people much smarter than me.

The 4% Rule

If you've visited any FIRE blogs, you've probably heard this term before. The 4% rule is famous in the financial community. When you flip this number around, it means you need roughly 25 times your annual spending in investments to retire. But how does it work?

The 4% rule comes from the famous Trinity Study in the US, which looked at different periods of history (including depressions, World Wars, high/low inflation and high/low interest rates) to see what a retiree could sustainably spend from their investments without running out of money. Using a portfolio of shares and bonds, it was found that in the worst-case scenario, a 4% withdrawal rate would have sustained a 30-year retirement in almost every possible scenario. Thus, 4% was deemed the 'safe withdrawal rate'.

But what if we're retired for more than 30 years? Well, the numbers aren't very different. Longer periods of retirement typically mean you want to have more of your money in shares to produce a better outcome, since shares outperform other asset classes over time.

Still, there are lots of assumptions built into the study. And plenty of arguments why the 4% rule is too optimistic or too conservative. The truth is, nobody knows the future. But if you take the practical approach I'll outline in this book, 4% is a simple and sensible guide in the right hands.

(For more on this topic, you'll find a podcast on the book resources page at: strongmoneyaustralia.com/bookextras - it's a special page you can visit for additional content and useful resources.)

Examples of the 4% Rule and Portfolio Size

Using the 4% rule, we can take a given level of annual spending and multiply it by 25. Here's how much savings you need to retire based on different levels of spending.

- $30,000 per year = $750,000
- $40,000 per year = $1 million
- $60,000 per year = $1.5 million
- $80,000 per year = $2 million
- $100,000 per year = $2.5 million
- $200,000 per year = $5 million

For every $1,000 of annual spending, you need an extra $25,000 of investments. This sounds like a lot. But honestly, don't worry too much about the numbers right now. It's likely your spending will be lower than you think once you see how simple it is to optimise.

And remember, if you have a paid-off home when you retire, your expenses will be lower than they are now. Personally, our expenses hover around $45,000 per year (including a mortgage), so we needed a little over $1 million to retire. We've got that covered, plus we're flexible spenders and earn some part-time income these days, so there's plenty of cushion in our situation.

The biggest mistake people make is thinking they need to be super rich to work less and live a more satisfying existence. In reality, you can create freedom with far less wealth than you think. Especially if you're interested in working part-time, which most people are. We'll talk more about dealing with market volatility later, but for now just understand that the more worried and rigid you are, the more cushion and investments you'll need. However, if you're flexible, the 4% rule is a comfy guide. We'll discuss living off an investment portfolio in practice later in this book.

How Long Does It Take To Become Financially Independent?

Your timeframe for achieving financial freedom is defined by one factor: your savings rate.

Your savings rate is the percentage of your after-tax income that you save. If you bring home $60,000 and save $6,000, your savings rate is 10%. If you save $15,000, your savings rate is 25%.

Here's the truth: if you never save, you'll never be financially independent. Well, aside from winning lotto or having wealthy parents dump a bunch of investments into your lap.

Without good savings habits, you'll be stuck at work forever, or at least until the pension kicks in.

However, as soon as you start saving and investing, your mandatory working period gets shorter. And the more you save, the shorter it becomes. The combination of saving (keeping your money) and investing (growing your money) is a powerful force.

As your savings and investments grow, there's a tipping point when your investments will provide enough returns for you to live on.

Let's put some numbers to it. Starting from scratch, here's how long it takes to reach FI, depending on your savings rate and using the 4% rule.

(Assumes 5% returns after inflation, with all returns reinvested, starting from zero. Some years are rounded for simplicity)

Savings Rate	Years to Retirement
95%	1.3
90%	2.7
85%	4
80%	5.5
75%	7
70%	8.5
65%	10
60%	12
55%	14
50%	16.5
45%	19
40%	21
35%	25
30%	28
25%	32
20%	37
15%	43
10%	51
5%	66

This is a simplified example, but it's a good illustration. Each time you level up on the savings rate ladder, it brings your freedom forward by years. *Many years.* Especially when you're starting on the lower rungs of the ladder.

Moving your savings rate from 20% to 25% brings your FI date closer by *five whole years.* An example of this is a household earning $100,000 and spending $80,000. If they can live on $75,000 instead, they create five extra years of freedom. That's a huge payoff for a small change.

However, there's a diminishing return. When you move from a 60% to 65% savings rate, you can retire 2 years earlier. Still incredible, but not quite as impactful as the first example.

Think about what this table means. If you start saving half your income in your early 20s, you can be FI by age 40. That leaves you with roughly another 60 years to do anything you like. If you start in your 30s, you'll be done by 50, with another 50 years of glorious freedom in your future.

Personally, our savings rate maxed out around 70-75%. That might sound absurd to you. But most people can save more than they think. Spending and saving are skills that we can improve. The problem is that we don't learn these things in school. Usually, we just copy habits from our peer group. However, once you start fine-tuning your savings skills, you'll be stunned at the impact. How can you improve your savings rate? There's two ways: earning more, and spending less. We'll discuss both, but first, let's start with why saving is so powerful.

Saving Builds Wealth

For years, I believed maximising my investment returns was the most important step in becoming financially independent.

The truth is that financial independence is built on a strong savings rate. Looking back, that was certainly true for my partner and I. We didn't make incredible investments, but we had great savings habits.

Let's say a couple earns a combined $100,000 per year. They want to retire early, so they optimise their spending and live on $50,000 per year. The other $50,000 is saved and invested.

Assuming a solid investment return of 7% per year, after 10 years, they'd have $720,000. A couple more years and they'll be a millionaire couple. Nice! But of this $720,000, only $220,000 came from investment returns.

Growth Over Time

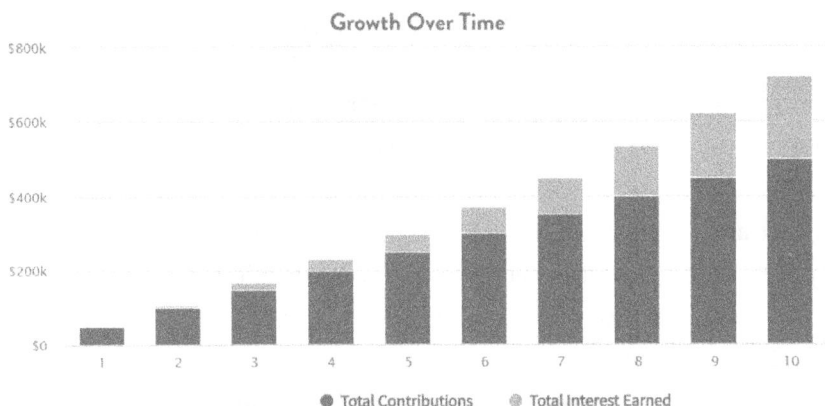

A whopping $500,000 came from their regular savings. That's about 70% of their total wealth!

Let's expand the timeframe and look at their whole FI journey, which would take 16–17 years from scratch.

After 17 years, your total balance is **$1,625,266**

Growth Over Time

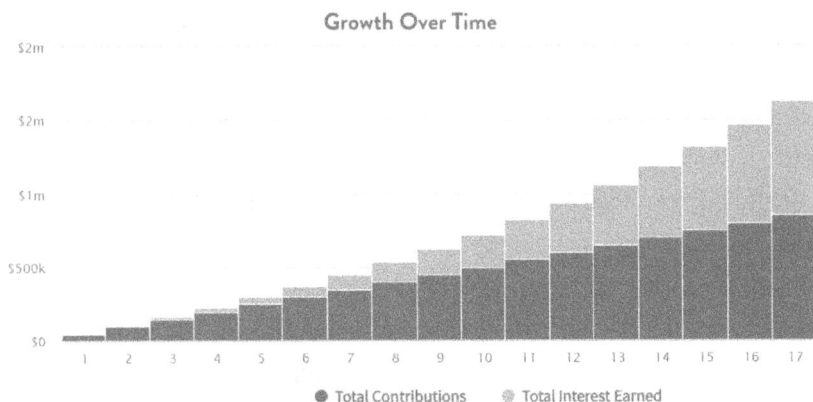

Now the investments are really starting to shine. By year 17, our couple has invested $850,000 of savings. Investment returns have added $775,000. So, even now, saving has created more than half of their wealth. Our couple can now generate around $65,000 in yearly income from this portfolio to cover their spending (which would now be higher due to inflation).

By the way, if we roll this forward, investing returns overtake savings at year 19.

I get this is counter intuitive. Most of us think investing is where the magic happens. That's true later, once you have a large portfolio. But compounding takes a long time. In the beginning, even the first 10-20 years, saving is MUCH more important.

Bottom line: saving more means reaching our goals faster. The more we save, the more we can invest. This builds our net worth quicker and gets that snowball rolling sooner. When people hear that saving is the magic ingredient in becoming FI, they sometimes become disheartened. Instead, I found this incredibly motivating. Here's why...

Saving is Within Your Control

We can't control how our investments perform. You can research all you like and obsess over the details every day. But you can't be certain of the result. While we can estimate long term returns, they aren't guaranteed.

Saving, on the other hand, is controllable. If we save $100 this week, it's there in our account until we use it. If we save more by increasing our income or cutting our expenses, more cash will pile up. Guaranteed payoff. We can do this over and over again, and it'll always work.

Alright, so we can see the power of saving. But maybe you don't want to save and invest for the next 10-20 years to be financially independent. Well, I have great news! You can achieve most of the benefits of FI in a much shorter time. Enter: semi-retirement, or what we'll call Semi-FI.

Semi-Retirement (AKA Semi-FI)

Instead of waiting until you have enough investments to live off completely, you can retire sooner and live *partly* off your investments. At this point, you either have a paid-off home or a decent portfolio generating some income, but not enough to live off.

To cover the rest of your spending, you simply do some part-time work. While it's not quite as sexy and exciting as complete freedom, let's look at the benefits:

- More freedom sooner. You need less to semi-retire and move away from full-time employment.
- You'll have more days off than you work. Even if you work 2 days per week, you get a 5-day weekend every single time!
- Most people are likely to earn money after retiring early anyway. This may be hard to envision right now, but it's almost certain to be true.
- You get the confidence, mindset, and lifestyle of someone who is fully FI, yet you only have to do a small amount of work to keep everything humming along.
- Less shock to your system than going from 100% work to 0%. Semi-retirement can act as a stepping stone, letting you taste freedom without such a big leap.
- You'll still become 100% FI over time if you maintain a small surplus and keep slowly adding to your investments.
- Some people don't want to stop working. You may like your job and simply want to work less and have more free time. Semi-FI is perfect for that.
- Due to earning less, you'll be on a low tax rate. Each hour of work will earn you more after-tax than before. This uses your time more efficiently and effectively gives you a pay-rise for working less.

So How Much Do You Need to Semi-Retire?

A great starting point for semi-retirement is when you have half your expenses covered by investment income. Or, alternatively, having a paid-off home, because in many cases a mortgage represents 35-50% of household expenses.

This level of financial strength is a good foundation to escape the rat race and transition into a cushy-yet-still-productive lifestyle. Also, knowing in your mind that half your expenses are covered by investments – or that you're mortgage-free – is a meaningful achievement, psychologically and financially.

Getting to the half-way point might seem arbitrary. But it offers a genuine lifestyle and happiness boost! We'll call this **the 50% rule.**

Let's consider a household who spends $50,000 per year. Half of this is their mortgage or rent, while the rest is personal expenses. Their FI goal is $1.25m. But what if they follow our 50% rule?

Rather than needing 25x their annual spending to retire, they only need 12.5x.

In this case, $625,000 (or a mortgage-free home) will do the job. Both options will mean half their expenses are covered, and they're in a great position to semi-retire.

With a little effort, most middle-class Aussies currently working full-time can achieve semi-FI in ten years. Hell, many will even achieve complete FI. And the earlier you start, the better this is. I have specific advice for late starters further on in this book. But the younger you are, the bigger the opportunity.

With the above example, our semi-retired household can now turn the dial more towards 'life' and activities of their choosing, with less reliance on employment income. However, they do still have a spending gap of $25,000 per year. How can they deal with this?

Covering the Gap

Our semi-retirees need to find $25,000 per year from somewhere. Ideally, a little more than that so they can keep growing their investments to strengthen their financial position over time. This is where part-time work comes in.

For a couple, it should be easy to earn $25,000 per year. At $25 per hour, this equates to roughly 20 hours of work per week, or just 10 hours each. At the median hourly wage ($36 per hour), it's less than 2 days of work per week (1 day each).

I should mention here that lower spenders have a built-in advantage. Why? The lower your expenses, the less part-time work you need.

All this is fantastic news for semi-retirees. It means the work doesn't need to be lucrative or high paying. Instead, you can find more meaningful, enjoyable work, rather than optimising just for money.

Other Ways to Semi-Retire

Another option is to scale down work as your investments grow over time. This won't be suitable for everyone due to workplace requirements, but it's worth keeping in mind. Imagine you build investments of $300,000, giving you a passive income of $12,000 per year. At this point, you could probably afford to drop a day at work each week.

If you maintain a savings surplus and add to your investments, you'll soon be able to afford two days off. Then three, and so on... until you're completely financially independent.

This option suits people who are generally happy with their careers, and just looking for extra freedom while still building their wealth. Another idea is to build some savings, then switch to part-time work (AKA cruise mode). You live solely off your part-time income while letting your investments compound in the background, eventually taking you to 100% FI.

These are all fantastic options, but note the trade-off: more free time sooner, while needing to work longer overall.

The 50% Rule and Spending

My wonderful-but-completely-made-up 50% rule says the ideal time to semi-retire is when your investments cover half your spending. The household who spends $50,000 per year needs $1.25m to fully retire, and $625,000 to semi-retire.

Now, let's say they'd been saving and investing for a while and had built up $500,000. This is 40% of their target, and 80% of the way to semi-FI. But maybe they decide to re-examine their lifestyle. They conclude that $40,000 per year would be enough for the life they want. This cuts the amount of savings they need to retire.

Now their FI goal is $1m. And their semi-FI target drops to $500,000. This means their progress instantly jumps. Now they're 50% towards FI, and can semi-retire now!

Constantly re-visiting and questioning our wants and needs is one of the best things we can do. Once we turn away from the standard consumer culture, and see how enslaving and unsatisfying it is, we often find desires melting away over time.

You could also approach semi-retirement another way: retire on the basics, and use part-time work to pay for luxuries. This mental framework is useful, especially those planning a higher spending retirement. It gives our brains a healthy message that luxuries require extra time and energy to attain. This helps us make clearer choices.

Final Thoughts on Semi-Retirement

Semi-FI is the ultimate solution for those who aren't wedded to the all-or-nothing approach to Financial Independence. And for those planning to keep working part-time anyway, semi-retirement is ideal.

Remember, if you structure your finances right and maintain a cashflow surplus, your wealth will keep growing, leading to complete FI later down the track. Semi-FI is hugely underutilised, and people often overestimate how much they need to achieve it.

It can give you ample free time, allowing you to live a great lifestyle, while staying engaged and productive, all with a respectable pot of savings looking after you in the background. So, if you're looking for a killer shortcut to freedom, maybe semi-retirement is for you.

Now that we've covered some of the numbers, let's discuss something equally important: the mindset.

The Importance of Our Values and Mindset

People with a focus on FI see things differently from the rest of society. Because despite the chatter about numbers and investing, our focus isn't really on the money at all.

Instead, we're playing a different game. And that shapes how we see the world and focus our energy. I've noticed many common ideals among myself and others on this path. Do you share any of the following traits or beliefs?

Independent thinking.

We tend to question the standard way things are done, and look for better alternatives. We enjoy finding solutions and finding new ways of looking at things (like how to live a great life at a much lower cost). We also tend to shrug off peer pressure and are more motivated by our own goals than 'fitting in'.

Time is our most precious resource.

Most people understand this is true, but we actually live it. We work smarter (and often harder) in the short term, to create as much future freedom as possible. Over the course of a good life, more of our time is better spent on more valuable things, rather than being trapped at the office/factory/worksite.

We see money as a game to win.

I find money fascinating. Not for the love of a dollar, but because it affects our lives so much. It's literally the reason people (reluctantly) get out of bed in the morning. Managing money is a skill we can become better at. And that skill has a huge payoff.

Our individual choices make a difference.

Our habits and lifestyle affect the planet in either a positive or negative way. High-consumption lifestyles have a huge environmental footprint, degrading the world for everyone else. Making choices which are better for the planet often align perfectly with our financial goals.

A high payback job is better than a high paying job.

In the short term, earning tons of money at work is fantastic, but later it won't mean as much. Financial independence allows you to choose work based on satisfaction, rather than salary. You can do work that means something to you, regardless of what it pays, or whether it even pays at all.

Embracing responsibility gives you power.

Your current situation might not be ideal. But you decide what happens next. Many are busy complaining how hard life is, how expensive things are, and how everything is outside their control. Far better to own your decisions – good and bad – and realise that your finances and future are largely determined by your choices.

There's no substitute for taking action.

Many wait for opportunities. Many wait for the perfect time to invest. Or until they're earning more to start saving. But the time to start is always right now. We can make things happen by taking small, regular steps towards our goals. Each step builds progress and momentum, which encourages more action.

Status and possessions are empty goals.

Many people are (often subconsciously) driven by these factors, though few will admit it. I definitely was in my early 20s. But even if we attain our desired luxuries, we won't be satisfied. There's always another level of opulence to reach. Always someone richer than you. Always another way to elevate your lifestyle. Always another net worth goal to reach. Recognising the unwinnable nature of the status and possessions game is the only true way to win.

Happiness is possible with very little.

Right now, there are plenty of people who are genuinely happy without the mountain of luxuries you have. That's because a happy life is not something you buy, but something you create. Chasing more consumer goods and exotic experiences isn't necessary, and can take away from our freedom and day-to-day enjoyment.

Or, as Jim Carrey put it: *"I think everybody should get rich and famous and do everything they ever dreamed of so they can see that it's not the answer."*

Alright, I may have just opened a can of worms with that last point. There is often some push-back here due to The Big Assumption: **spending less means a less enjoyable life.**

Spending, Happiness, and Financial Independence

Our goal is to build a satisfying life, without spending *all* our money, so that we can save and invest to create more freedom for ourselves. How do we do that? First, let's consider why we spend money in the first place.

Clearly, if we spent no money, we'd have complete freedom right now. But that's not realistic, is it? As humans, we have very natural wants and needs.

We want to own things. Maybe a nice home and some furniture. A car or a bike. Decent clothes. A phone and computer. Possibly some artwork. Jewellery. On and on. But that's just possessions. What about our lifestyle?

We want to spend our free time doing enjoyable things. That could include visiting a new place, heading out to a sports event, or maybe just sitting at the beach and sipping a coffee. All great stuff.

But which of these things is truly worthwhile? What actually makes a person happy and fulfilled?

The Science of Happiness

Luckily for us, people have studied happiness for decades. And while it's true that we're all individuals with different personalities, there's strong similarities in what makes for a satisfying existence. Here's what comes up again and again:

- A safe and comfortable place to live
- Good relationships and sense of community
- Low stress
- Good physical and mental health
- Feeling in control of our lives
- Contribution through helping others or causes we care about
- Having meaningful work

- Being financially secure
- A sense of independence and freedom

And what makes someone unhappy? The opposite.

An unsafe environment. Strained relationships. High stress. Poor physical and mental health. No freedom or control. Having nothing to contribute to. Work that's draining. And being in poor financial shape.

Here's two questions to consider:

Do the above things cost a lot of money? Not really. We can make them expensive, but they don't have to be.

Does financial independence help or harm these goals? Clearly, it has a huge positive influence on these things.

FI is empowering in each area. Financial security, obviously! A lower stress lifestyle. More time for your health and relationships. A definite sense of freedom and control. Easier to contribute to things and find more engaging or meaningful work to do.

Do you see how all this comes together? By understanding the relationship between happiness, spending and wealth, we can make positive changes in our lives, knowing we'll be just as happy and better off for it. Maybe even happier!

In other words, financial independence helps us break down barriers to happiness by removing certain frustrations and pains from our lives, empowering us to focus on doing more fulfilling things.

With a large portion of our wellbeing built on good health, relationships, and spending time doing things that feel meaningful, there aren't many things you can buy to 'enhance' your life.

In fact, thinking about *quality of life* in terms of yearly spending often takes you down the wrong path.

When do you feel truly happy? Often, the simpler things are what comes to mind. Laughing with a friend. Those quiet moments with your spouse. Pausing to marvel at the ocean or the stars. Exploring on a camping trip. The challenge of vigorous exercise.

Yes, money helps with certain things. But 'dollars spent' is a terrible gauge for how fulfilling a life is. Many times, big spenders are the least fulfilled people. Which makes sense when you think about it. They feel something is missing, that things could be better. So they chase consumer highs and fancier experiences.

In contrast, when you feel satisfied with your life, you feel nothing is lacking. And with that contentment, the urge to spend money melts away. There are no emotional gaps to fill. Now, some studies have shown a link between increased income and increased happiness, which tends to taper off once we hit middle class full-time wages.

But you know why I think this link exists? Not because more spending makes us happier. But because a higher income gives us more options. And that makes us feel more in control of our lives. So when our money situation is good, that feeling of empowerment and control is what gives us a greater sense of life satisfaction.

Perhaps counterintuitively, even if your goal was to spend as much as humanly possible over the course of your entire life, you can best do that by spending less today and investing the difference for as long as possible. The money you invest will multiply itself many times over the course of decades, giving you far more total spending power than if you spend those dollars as soon as they come in. More on this phenomenon of compound interest in the next chapter.

The Fundamentals of FI

In this chapter, we covered a lot of ground...

- How much net investments you need to reach FI (25x expenses is a good guideline).
- The importance of your savings rate (and how long the journey will take depending on how much you save).
- Opting for semi-retirement to create freedom sooner with less savings.

- The values and mindset that help us achieve Financial Independence.
- What humans really need to be happy.

You don't need to be mega-rich to live with greater independence and do your own thing. You can do it with much less than most people think. For me, things changed when I had a mindset shift...

Instead of asking, "How much do I need to retire?" I started thinking, "How little do I need to retire?" This helped me question what I really needed, resulting in financial independence much sooner than expected.

Now that we've covered the fundamentals of how FI works, it's time to start working on our finances. We'll start with my favourite personal finance lessons.

4

Personal Finances + Getting Started

"Spending money to show people how much money you have is the fastest way to have less money." - *Morgan Housel*

Now that you know the basics of FI, you're ready to put yourself in a strong financial position.

But how do we structure our finances to make this happen?

In this chapter, we'll discuss how to build financial habits to set you up for success. Having a solid financial foundation is a key first step, because there's no point in investing until our personal finances are in great shape.

You're about to learn:

- Timeless personal finance lessons that will benefit you for the rest of your life.
- How to take stock of your current situation.
- My thoughts on budgets and buckets (and how I manage my money).
- How to make better financial decisions.
- The most important first steps to take (like what to do with your first $10,000).

Now, I know we haven't covered super actionable things to do yet. We will!

First, I want to give you the operating manual for *how to think about your finances* and adapt these lessons into your own life. Because this is what many books ignore. They simply give you a set of arbitrary steps and instructions which are somehow the same for everyone.

But when you have the mindset and principles down, you don't need to follow somebody else's instructions. You know what to do, why to do it, and how to adjust course when required. I'll share everything you need to know, but your life, finances, values and goals are your own, which is why I won't give you a one-size-fits-all, cookie-cutter approach.

With that out of the way, let's get stuck into my favourite personal finance lessons. This stuff gets me all warm and fuzzy inside like a giddy child on Christmas morning.

Lesson 1: Saving is the Secret

Yep, I'm hammering this point home, and for good reason! Because here's the thing: you can receive millions of dollars and still end up broke.

In fact, most people will earn millions of dollars throughout their lives. An employee earning $70,000 after tax will have $1 million pass through her bank account in just 15 years. Pretty crazy, right? Multiply that over a lifetime.

Now, of course, we need to pay for housing, food, and other stuff. I'm not saying we should all be instant millionaires. But a lot of money comes our way over the years, and it's up to us how much we keep. Consider the countless celebrities and sports stars who have earned obscene money during their careers, only to end up completely bankrupt, with crippling debts.

There's no amount of money that can't be spent. As soon as one desire is satisfied, another one pops up. Once they have a Lamborghini, now they need a yacht. Once they have a high-end penthouse, now they need a country estate. It's like some sick consumer version of the game whack-a-mole.

And while their career is booming, their earnings easily cover these costs, and more – like permanent chefs, butlers, and one of those towel guys like in the bathroom of fancy restaurants, because, well, why not?

All this sounds ridiculous to normal people like us. But this happens to regular folks too, just on a smaller scale. As our income goes up, we usually match that with increased spending (remember the study of household spending in Chapter 2?).

So it's not how much we earn that matters. It's how much we save. Which leads into the next point.

Lesson 2: The Wealth Illusion

If someone has an expensive car, takes luxury holidays, or has a fancy house, this tells us nothing about their wealth. In reality, all it takes is a good income to qualify for loans.

Thanks to social media, people are trying to project the appearance of wealth and success more than ever. But looks can be deceiving. Most people that look rich probably aren't.

If someone has expensive things, it doesn't mean they *have* a lot of money. It means they've *spent* a lot of money. Which, when you think about it, is basically the opposite of having a lot of money.

Now sure, both can be true. But in many cases, it's not. While someone can look rich, they may have little or no wealth. For me, this message sank in while reading *The Millionaire Next Door,* by Thomas Stanley and William Danko. It's a fantastic book which studied a large group of US millionaires (from all sorts of ethnicities and backgrounds).

As it turns out, the average millionaire doesn't live in a high-end suburb. Nor do they typically drive expensive cars. These are wealthy people who live well, but they prioritise saving and building up investments or businesses. I remember having an epiphany while reading the book: basically, we get two choices with our money. We can spend it trying to *look* rich. Or we can invest it to *become* rich. I decided the second option made more sense.

People will not like you better for your stuff. Don't waste your time with status symbols to win approval from others. As one of my favourite writers Mark Manson said: *"You'll stop caring what other people think of you when you have something more important to care about."*

Lesson 3: Compound Interest

Einstein called compound interest the Eighth Wonder of the World, because it's truly incredible.

Let's say $1,000 is invested for a child upon birth and they can receive it as a prize for reaching age 100. No money is ever added to the initial investment. What do you think this $1,000 would grow into? $5,000? $30,000? $90,000?

Try $1 million. Yep, with a return of 7.2% per year, money doubles roughly every ten years.

- Year 0: $1,000
- Year 10: $2,000
- Year 20: $4,000
- Year 30: $8,000
- Year 40: $16,000
- Year 50: $32,000
- Year 60: $64,000
- Year 70: $128,000
- Year 80: $256,000
- Year 90: $512,000
- Year 100: $1,024,000

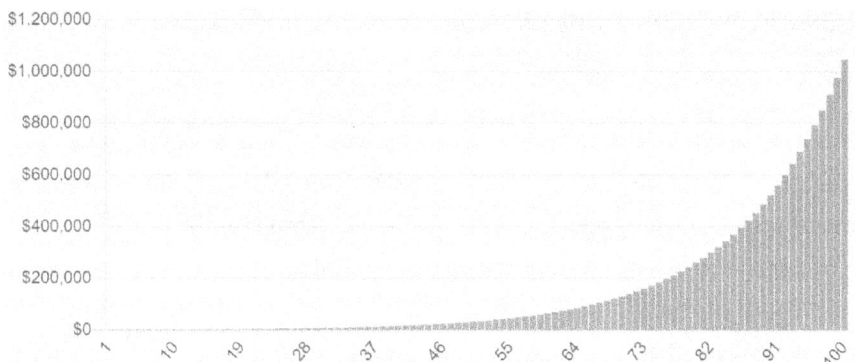

Notice how half the wealth was created in the last ten years. And three quarters have come in the last 20 years. It looks like nothing is happening, and then the value explodes. That's the catch: it takes a long time to create explosive results.

When I first read about compound interest, I must have stared at the page for an hour, unable to believe what I was seeing. Almost instantly, spending became far less attractive to me, and investing became fascinating. The way money multiplies over time just blew my mind, and still does to this day.

As amazing as it is, most people are blind to the power of compound interest. Even if you're only half good with money, yet you understand compounding, it's almost impossible not to become a millionaire over time.

Here's why: Invest $500 a month at a 7% annual return, and you'll have around $1.3 million in 40 years. Now imagine what the numbers look like when you invest $500 *per week*, or more. The numbers start getting silly. But instead of working until we're filthy rich, this book is about having 'enough' to help us shift our focus towards other things.

Someone who truly understands compounding is legendary investor Warren Buffett. He's worth over $100 billion as I write this. And 99% of his wealth came after age 50 (he's in his 90s now). Because that's just how compounding works. The longer time goes on, the more insane compounding looks.

Start saving and investing as soon as possible and your future self will be glad you did.

Lesson 4: Spending Dictates Your Freedom

Many 'free spenders' are anything but free. Their spending and debt effectively controls them. High spenders are generally more stressed, because they need to keep generating a large income to stay afloat.

Their life may look glitzy, with designer clothes, fancy cars, and exotic holidays, but there's little chance of taking a break from the workforce in the short term. And they need to work longer to save enough to retire in the long term.

> "People who live far below their means enjoy a freedom that people busy upgrading their lifestyle can't fathom." – *Naval Ravikant*

In my experience, high spenders are also far more worried about having 'enough'. Now, there are always people with large incomes who spend extravagantly and still manage to become wealthy. But these are few and far between.

Most of us must use our limited resources wisely. Lower spending makes it easier to reach FI, which leads to more freedom sooner, and lower stress levels along the way.

Money is a tool that gives you options. It can be used for many things. Having money is far better than not having it. And spending it is the fastest way to not have it. So *not saving* is the best way to rob yourself of optionality.

During my journey, it became clear that if we could live on less than our peers, we could gain our freedom relatively quickly. And that's exactly what happened. It wasn't necessarily hard, just different. But it's why I'm sitting here in my early 30s writing to you on a sunny Perth day, instead of being stuck at work.

I should admit something here. Initially, we did plan on living a more materialistic life than we have today. We wanted freedom, yes, but we also wanted (eventually) to have new cars, a fancy waterfront house, and plenty of spending money. But as time went on, we realised this level of wealth would require many more years of working and investing. Not only that, but we noticed we'd become happier despite our spending falling over the years (we'll talk about how to live a good life for less in the next two chapters!).

So why bother sacrificing another ten years for a fancier lifestyle? Gaining freedom was much more valuable. Which connects to something else I want to reinforce.

Lesson 5: A Happy Life Doesn't Require a Lot of Money

In my view, this factor impacts the personal finances of everyday Aussies more than anything else. By failing to recognise this truth, we end up chasing our tails and blowing our bank accounts, thinking we can find happiness in consumption, status, or luxury. But it's just a story we tell ourselves.

If you only take one thing from this whole book, I hope it's this. Because once you internalise this message, you'll no longer stress about having enough money. You'll also become financially independent much faster. Then, from your position of freedom, you can decide whether it's worth scaling up the spending for a little more luxury.

Otherwise, higher spending habits become hard to wind back. We simply become accustomed to our lifestyle, no matter how luxurious it becomes. Remember hedonic adaptation?

Having freedom is more satisfying than anything else I could spend money on. There are many ways we could spend more, but almost none of them will make our lives permanently better or more meaningful.

The truth is, a happy life doesn't cost much. Part of that is because we live in modern-day Australia, so we already have incredible living standards. However, a lot of us don't feel wealthy because we compare ourselves to the tiny percentage of people who are even better off, rather than the billions of global citizens who are poorer than us.

Most of us simply lucked into being alive in Australia today. We couldn't choose which year we were born, which country we were born in, or where our parents migrated to. However we got here, we can choose to live great lives without spending *all* of our income.

Some people suggest that saving means a life of 'sacrifice'. But think of it this way: **you're not sacrificing your spending so that you can save. You're sacrificing your freedom so that you can spend.**

Lesson 6: You Control Money, or Money Controls You

Money has a big role in our lives, whether we like it or not. But how we deal with this can vary massively. For many of us, our relationship with money is like an ongoing power struggle. In fact, we spend most of our waking hours doing some type of money-earning activity.

We sacrifice time with our loved ones and pets, ignore our hobbies and passions, and sometimes even our health, because we have no choice but to work. Still, you might say that money doesn't control you. After all, you're making the decisions, right?

You choose which car to buy. You pick which restaurant to eat at. You even decide how many doves to release at little Emily's princess-themed 2nd birthday party, which she barely knows is happening, definitely won't remember, and (if we're totally honest) is more about us showing off on social media.

It seems like we're in control. But we're going back to work on Monday, often for a job we don't like. Why? Because we need the money. So it's fair to say that money has complete control over how we spend our time. That is, unless we do something about it. We can learn to make our money work hard, so that eventually, we don't have to work at all.

How Long Will It Take To Become a Millionaire?

Here's how long it will take to reach seven figures, depending on how much you invest. This assumes you're starting from zero and have 7% annual returns.

- $500/month: 37 years.
- $1,000/month: 28 years.
- $2,000/month: 20 years.
- $3,500/month: 14 years.
- $5,000/month: 11 years.
- $7,500/month: 8 years.

Put another way, here's what you'd have after 20 years of investing different amounts.

- $500/month: $260,463.
- $1,000/month: $520,927.
- $2,000/month: $1,041,853.
- $3,500/month: $1,823,243.
- $5,000/month: $2,604,633.
- $7,500/month: $3,906,950.

As you can see, the more you can invest, the faster you'll join the Double-Comma-Club and hit millionaire status! The result multiplies by how much you put into it. Now, it's possible you need more than a million bucks depending on your situation. But I hope the example is clear. If those big numbers seem intimidating, don't worry. In the next few chapters, you'll learn how to save tons of cash while still living well.

Taking Stock of Where You Are

Okay, now let's get a handle on your current situation. What financial shape are you in?

Once we know where we are, we can start making the right moves towards a wealthier future.

Write down the values of the following:

- Bank accounts and savings accounts.
- Share investment accounts (any brokerage accounts or investing apps).
- Any rental property you own (minus the value of the mortgage).

These are your true *investment assets*. This is wealth that can be used to generate passive income to live on right now. Next, write down the value of the following assets. These may become significant factors in your FI plans, depending on your situation.

- The home you live in (minus the value of the mortgage).
- Your superannuation accounts.

Now, add it all up. Deduct the value of any car loans, personal loans and credit card balances. This is your total net worth. Is this more or less than you thought?

It doesn't matter where you are right now, but it's good to be aware of this number.

Because our focus here is on financial independence, how we look at assets and wealth is a little different. Having equity in our home is great, but unless the home is paid off, this doesn't increase our freedom.

Likewise, having a beefed up superannuation fund is fantastic, but if we're 35 years old, we have to wait until our 60s to actually benefit from it. It does nothing for our freedom today.

We'll dive deeper into mortgages and super later, but for now, understand this: where you park your dollars has a huge impact on your ability to live a more self-directed life. All net worth is not equal.

In simple terms, there are two metrics that matter the most:

- Passive income from investments.
- Your annual expenses.

Our job is simply to close the gap between these two numbers.

The most effective way to do that is by increasing our investments and decreasing our expenses. But maybe you aren't sure how much you spend each year. In this case, we need to figure that out immediately, since everything revolves around this number. It comes back to the multiplier effect. Because you need 25x your annual spending in investments to retire, as your spending changes, it has a 25x effect on how much you need.

How to Track Your Spending

One eye-opening way to figure out your average expenses is to record everything you spend money on for about 3 months. In fact, it's a great habit to track your spending even when your finances are in good shape. It's always interesting to see it laid out in front of you.

While this sounds as fun as living on brussels sprouts, there are many ways to get a good handle on your expenses. With the options I'm about to share, you're bound to find a system that works for you, and – most importantly – doesn't make you want to burn your bank cards and never think about money again.

Don't skip this. Without knowing how much you spend, your financial success will come down to luck. And you're probably reading this to take control of your life, not to rely on luck.

You might even like to treat this like a game. Pretend it's someone else's spending you get to spy on. You're a detective who must uncover clues as to what this person does and where their money goes. It'll probably feel like someone else's spending, anyway. Why? Because you'll likely find items in your transaction history that you won't even remember! This even happens to me, and I've got a blackbelt in frugality.

As for how to track your spending, there's a few ways. If you're old school, you can set up a simple spreadsheet. Create a list of categories down one side, with the months of the year listed across the top. One day each week, enter and update your spending amounts for each category according to your bank transactions for the previous 7 days. After a few months, you'll start to get a good idea where your money is going. I follow this simple approach and it takes about 5 minutes per week.

If that's not your style, you could try one of the many spending tracker apps which have become more popular in recent years. Some banking apps will also categorise your spending for you.

The important thing is to find a 'money management strategy' that works for you. As I see it, there are four main approaches to choose from.

Budgeting

Lots of people hate this. Look, I hear you. I've never actually followed a budget myself. Having confined amounts of money for each category of life seems rigid and unnecessary. But budgets can work for some people.

Personally, I learned to simply question each item of spending to see whether it was worth sacrificing my hard-earned dollars. Since each expense is taking away from our freedom, it had better be worth it.

As you go down this path, you might find that investing your money brings you more pleasure than spending it, because you know it's building another chunk of future freedom. Still, in the beginning, a budget might be exactly what you need.

How do you know if you need a budget? Well, if there's money in your account, do you immediately start thinking about what you could buy? If so, maybe a budget is the right approach. Get all your expenses written down by following the previous step. How does it look? What stands out? Which areas can be improved?

There are countless ways you can draw up a budget which I won't dwell on here, but the savings ideas in the coming chapters will hopefully inspire you to see where you can optimise and plan your budget accordingly (if you choose this method).

Buckets

Bucketing is a simple approach where you set aside certain percentages of your pay for different things. For example, 30% for housing, 30% for other living costs, 20% for spending, 10% for savings, 10% for investing.

Bucketing often involves having a string of different accounts for various things. One for basics, one for short-term savings, one for short-term spending, and another for long-term goals.

As with budgeting, this forces us to limit our spending in certain areas. For example, when there's no money left in our spending account, that's it until the next payday. It's easy to see why this works.

But these numbers are also arbitrary. More concerningly, they always include a dedicated account for wasting money. I can't get on board with that because we often feel compelled to spend it since it's already carved out for us. Unfortunately, nobody tackles the tricky question: does this spending actually make me happier?

Other books don't discuss this because it's easier to get people excited by 'guilt-free spending'. I get that. But I'd rather share some honest truths. And breaking the consumption = happiness myth is an important lesson.

Even though it works, bucketing feels a bit like ten-pin bowling with the guardrails up. It'll make you head in the right direction, but ultimately, it's better to take those guardrails down and develop the skills to guide the ball yourself.

These first two approaches are ideal for beginners or those simply wanting to build financial security. But for creating financial *freedom*, we need a different playbook. The next two approaches are far more flexible and empowering.

The Save-first Principle

Paying yourself first – or the 'save-first' principle – means setting money aside as soon as you get paid, before you spend a dollar on anything else.

Say you earn $1,000 per week. With this approach, you might set aside $200 automatically on payday, via direct debit. This avoids having to rely on memory or discipline each time! The cash is used to build savings, pay down debt, or invest.

You're then free to use the rest of your income as you please, spending more in areas that are more important and less on what isn't. What I like about this is that saving comes before everything else. It's also simpler because you only need one main bank account.

Plus, as you become used to saving the set amount, it can be boosted slightly on a regular basis. After a month, increase your weekly automatic savings from $200 to $220 and you'll barely even notice. This process can be repeated as we become accustomed to living on what's left after saving.

Over time, as our income and savings habit builds, we'll be tucking away a bigger percentage of our pay than we ever thought possible. Try going from saving nothing to half of your pay and it'll be a huge lifestyle change. You'll almost certainly fail. But try increasing your savings rate by 1% each month. Easy!

Mindful Spending

Mindful spending simply means deliberate or intentional spending. It means taking note of where our money is going (which we learn from tracking). Then we sit down and question each category to consider how much benefit we're getting from those dollars. It's a philosophical approach to managing money.

More than anything, it's about building the habit of questioning why you're doing what you're doing. Some people find that uncomfortable, but it's one of the most valuable skills you can develop, because it helps ensure your actions are aligned with your long-term goals.

I love this style of money management. From my experience, this strategy leads to the highest levels of saving without feelings of missing out (because it's all by design). Now, this doesn't mean you agonise over every decision. That would be exhausting. It means you build the habit of self-reflection, and considering whether you're happy about where your dollars are going.

Can I get the same benefit at a lower cost? Is this new thing really worth buying? Do I need to do this activity as often? Are there better deals on this product or service? Is this something I genuinely enjoy or just a habit I've picked up? Essentially, it's an attitude of optimisation.

By developing this mindset over time, you prove to yourself that spending less simply means you're more efficient at meeting your needs. This doesn't mean watching every penny, either. Mindful spending can often lead to the point where, counterintuitively, you actually don't think about money very much. You either need something or you don't. Something is worth doing or it's not. And when bills come up or you happen to look at your spending, you think "is there a way to improve this?"

Takeaways

Your job is to decide which spending strategy will work best for you. That will depend on your personality and current habits. Remember, you can always test each approach and see which one feels right.

While I do think there are lifetime benefits in becoming a mindful spender or using the save-first approach, there's no one-size-fits-all answer.

Some people will say "I just want to never think about money". But that isn't very realistic. It often comes from someone who wants to spend a lot without any downside. This is what causes average people to be trapped in the rat race and what causes rich people to go broke. Managing our finances is something we can enjoy and even relish, because it gives us the power to create the life we want.

Why do I like mindful spending so much? The same reason I love Financial Independence. Freedom. Spend on anything you like, but it must pass a stringent filter first. Let me show you how I make spending decisions.

How to Make Better Financial Decisions

There are plenty of things that can add value to our lives. Some purchases not only give us daily joy, but also help us save time, save money, and even remove headaches from our life.

Here are just a few of the best things I've spent money on:

- Bicycle.
- Weights.
- Dog.
- French Press coffee maker.
- Comfortable bed.
- Reliable technology and internet.

Your list could include a musical instrument, gym membership, comfortable shoes, books, etc.

None of these things are necessarily expensive, especially considering how much use and benefits we can derive from these things over many years. Still, there's an important point here: just because a purchase seems like it would make our daily life better, this doesn't mean it gets an immediate green light.

Why not? Well, that framework is a slippery slope to justifying almost any expense. Let's be clear, feeling pain because you desire a new product is not a genuine pain-point. It's important to be honest with yourself.

What follows is a list of what runs through my mind (automatically at this point) when thinking about expenses. Over the years, mindful spending helped me see where money was leaking out of my life for no real benefit. The fact is, every purchase has consequences – some good, some bad.

Each of these points acts like a filter that catches poor decisions before they're made. The aim isn't perfection, but simply to be more focused and aware. Having a framework like this is incredibly useful, because when it comes to our personal finances, our decisions determine our destiny.

Financial Cost

Every expense lowers our bank balance, so there's a clear and immediate cost. Many purchases can be worthwhile, but depending on how we frame it, it's possible to justify almost anything. This means it pays to always question yourself.

If you're not yet financially independent, then every day that passes means you're giving up your freedom for that spending. And much of our spending isn't one-off, it's ongoing. That new shirt may feel like a random purchase, and the car only needs repairs every now and then. But we tend to always spend a certain amount on these seemingly random things every single year. In fact, when we zoom out, they're quite predictable.

Let's flesh this out further. If we need 25x our annual spending in investments to produce enough passive income to live off, a $50 weekly expense – $2,600 per year – has a true cost of $65,000. Because to produce $2,600 per year, we need $65,000 in investments. Looked at this way, some of your spending may terrify you, which might be a good thing! But rather than dwell on it, consider the opportunity.

For every $10 per week you can trim from your spending – $520 per year – that's $13,000 less you need in investments. You're essentially $13,000 closer to FI.

When I'm thinking about a purchase decision, I always consider the annual cost and multiply that by 25 to see how much investments we'd need to cover the ongoing expense. Many times, that's off-putting enough. Otherwise, I move to the next layer of my decision-making framework.

Happiness Outcome

The true goal behind our spending is to live a happy life. As it turns out, we're not very good at predicting what makes us happy. Humans have this in-built desire for more, which makes us always want something new, better, and different.

But the hedonic treadmill effect shows us we're suckers for believing it. We do that thing, buy that product, and eventually the initial burst of pleasure disappears and we feel the same as before.

So I try to think: will this make me any happier? Not just right now, but in a lasting way. Most of the time, the answer is no. It's easy to get short-term sugar-highs with a holiday or a new phone. But they don't last, leaving you back where you started, just a little poorer than you were before.

Remember, this doesn't mean you say no to the purchase. It just means you make a more educated decision without any rose-coloured assumptions about its effect on your life.

Environmental Effect

If you haven't heard, Australia (and the world) has a gut-wrenching problem with waste and pollution. After seeing shows like *War on Waste*, it's hard not to be disturbed by the consequences of our seemingly small actions.

As individuals, a plastic bottle, coffee cup or piece of clothing thrown out doesn't feel like much. But there's 25 million of us 'individuals' in this country alone! This means our habits as individuals create big issues as a nation. Saying "it's only me", or "it's only this small thing" just doesn't cut it. The problem with this attitude is, it causes millions (even billions) of people to think their actions don't matter, when the opposite is true.

We often like to blame governments and large corporations for society's problems, with waste being just one example. But that's just a lazy and convenient way to look at it. Governments and corporations are simply trying to give us what they think we want. Sure, they have power and need to be held accountable. But, ultimately, our votes and dollars determine their practices.

Nowadays, I try to think about what went into making something before buying it. Consider a t-shirt. It takes 2,700 litres of water, plus materials, transport, and factory pollution to produce. Most manufactured items we buy have been made in a factory spewing out smog. And almost everything is heavily wrapped in paper, cardboard, or plastic, contributing to deforestation and yet more waste. Then there's the transport involved: in the materials, in getting it to the ports, shipping it across countries, getting it to the shop, and us going to purchase it.

Before we get too depressed, realise that this is a difficult and inescapable fact of modern life. I'm not saying you should buy nothing. But we should be thoughtful about what we choose to buy and aware of the environmental costs.

Opportunity Cost

Opportunity cost is a fancy way of saying "what else could the money be used for?" For our purposes, one obvious choice is investing. Let's say you've got a 15-year timeframe until you reach FI and you're considering a car purchase. You could buy a decent second-hand car for $10,000. Your other choice is a newer, more luxurious car, costing $25,000.

Choosing the higher cost option, you may think the opportunity cost is $15,000. But because we're investing any surplus money, the $15,000 left over from the cheaper car purchase is worth more over time. In fact, after 15 years, it becomes $42,734.

None of the above is meant to guilt you into never buying anything. It's about seeing our spending in a more complete way. Because to achieve something great like financial independence, we need to take this shit seriously and think about the bigger picture. After all, even empires are built one brick at a time.

Freedom of Choice

In the modern world, almost everything is a choice. It might not feel that way sometimes, but it is. Where we work, where we live, *how* we live, what we spend time and money on – all are ongoing decisions. To keep everything the same is a choice to make zero changes.

We can choose to approach any aspect of our life differently than we currently do. We can wake up in the same place, eat the same food, go to the same job, buy the same things, talk to the same people, think the same thoughts. Basically, we can choose to live on autopilot. Or we can do something different.

If anything can be altered, then it's a choice. Most of the time, we dismiss change as impossible, when the truth is that it just feels too hard. The trick is to start with the smallest tweaks possible and go from there.

Just like you wouldn't peel yourself off the couch, stroll right into the gym and go pick up the heaviest weights, there's no need for you to completely upend your life all at once. You'd start in that gym with some light weights for a short session, just to show yourself you could do it. Then you can progress to harder weights as your confidence and strength grows.

Making small tweaks helps you remember that most things in your current life could be changed if you desired, and you can come out stronger on the other side.

The Most Important First Step

Regardless of your age or your income, there is one thing we all need: a cash cushion. It doesn't matter how secure you think your job is. You need access to cash in an emergency. Job loss, vet bills, car repairs, health problems. Things we may need thousands of dollars for at a moment's notice.

A cash cushion or emergency fund helps you sleep at night. If something happens, you know you'll be fine, financially speaking. This gives you huge peace of mind and a sense of security.

Without a cash cushion, people become trapped in a cycle of personal loans, high interest credit cards, and debt repayments. They put one fire out, another pops up, and around they go again. This is a financially vulnerable position to be in.

The opposite, of course, is financial strength: having quick access to a pile of money at a moment's notice. This emergency fund can take multiple forms:

- Cash in the bank (savings or offset account).
- Annual leave you would be paid in case of job loss (or that you can cash-out).
- A redraw facility in your home loan.

- Other liquid investments you can cash out quickly (like shares or bonds).
- Access to a very low/no interest credit card.

While they don't apply to everyone, all are potential ways to get cash quickly. My preferred option is old fashioned cash in the bank. Sure, it earns little, but its value is guaranteed, you can get it whenever you want, and there are no hurdles or risks like some of the other options.

How Much Cash Cushion Should You Keep?

Your emergency fund should be tailored to your situation. Imagine a two-person household, who are both working, renting, and have low expenses. Let's say they live on one income and save the other. In case of one spouse losing their job, this couple can carry on just fine.

Another household may have just one income earner, higher spending, multiple children, and a large house to maintain. They need more cushion. Costly home repairs and job loss could quickly create a sticky situation.

Personally, I think 3 months of expenses is a good starting point for most people. This means a household spending $60,000 per year would want to keep access to at least $15,000. If you already have a high savings rate, low expenses, income-producing investments, annual leave built up, and home equity you can redraw, you may be fine with less cash.

On the other hand, if you want to be conservative, keep more. Essentially, you want enough so that you don't have to worry. That's the whole point of the cash cushion. Cushions are supposed to be comfortable!

Don't go overboard though, as hoarding cash has diminishing benefits. Too much cash has a big opportunity cost, since it could be earning higher returns elsewhere.

Can I Earn More with My Cash Cushion?

There is no shortage of places to park your short-term savings. But remember: the purpose of this emergency fund is that it's for emergencies! The goal here is not high returns. It's stability and certainty.

This is your *safe* money, so keep it safe. Don't worry, your investments will do the heavy lifting when it comes to returns. There's no point investing every single dollar and then having to raid your investments for all of life's little problems. An emergency fund allows you to approach your investments with an 'own forever' mentality.

Your cash cushion is a simple yet powerful weapon. When one of those crappy random events happens, you can swat it away like a fly on your shoulder. This builds a strong base of financial strength.

Now it's time to kick things up a notch. Let's discuss how to supercharge your savings rate by tackling life's biggest expenses.

5

Big Wins to Supercharge Your Savings Rate

"Wealth consists not in having great possessions, but in having few wants." - *Epictetus*

We all want to live a great quality of life, while saving and investing a solid amount.

And we'd rather do it without living in a cardboard box beside the highway, living off roadkill, and drinking rainwater through our socks. Possible? Yes! And the way we do that is by approaching life's big expenses in a smarter, more thoughtful way.

The overarching principle here is not sacrifice. It's finding ways to create a satisfying life at a lower cost than your peers. And by mastering the skill of spending money effectively to get what you want for less, you're basically beating the system. In this chapter, I'll share plenty of strategies you can use to optimise the biggest costs we all face. You might be surprised how achievable this is.

Think of these like a list of ideas, not a set of orders. As long as you get to a nice savings rate overall, that's what matters.

We'll get to increasing your income later in this book. But it's important to sort our expenses first, so we can make the most of that extra income and use it wisely. Otherwise an increase in earnings will just increase our spending.

Where do we begin? Well, once your cash cushion is set up, the next step is to cut any consumer debt. Car loans, credit cards, personal loans, and more.

If you're already debt-free (aside from a mortgage, which we'll cover soon), congratulations! You can skip this step and go straight to 'housing'.

Remove All Consumer Debt from Your Life Forever

Paying off consumer debt and credit cards is usually the best return you'll ever make. If shares will earn a long-term return of 7% per year, paying off a credit card charging 20% per annum is a slam dunk. And paying off a personal or car loan which typically charges 5-10% interest is also a wise move at this point. It's a healthy, guaranteed return that's tax-free with no risk.

When the interest rate is below 5%, the choice is less clear. For a car loan, I would still opt to pay it off. Removing these repayments means you have lower monthly expenses, and makes your finances simpler to manage.

Some people say to pay down all personal debts before doing anything else. But I suggest you build your cash cushion first. Why? Well, when people try to pay off personal debts first, something inevitably happens, and their lack of a cash cushion means a new loan is needed, which starts the process all over again.

With that done, now it's time to tackle the big stuff. And what better place to start than with the elephant in the room: Aussie housing.

Aussie Housing

Regardless of where you live, housing is likely to be your biggest expense. For this reason, it deserves the most scrutiny. How can we find ourselves a nice place to live without breaking the bank?

To start with, you might be wondering "aren't house prices in Australia kind of a deal breaker when it comes to getting ahead, let alone retiring early?" The answer is no. It's a hurdle, sure, but not a dealbreaker. Your mortgage repayments and other ongoing costs are more important than actual house prices when it comes to building wealth.

Yes, house prices have gone up a lot over the last few decades. But thanks to interest rates being much lower now than in decades past (say 2 to 5% versus 8 to 20%) mortgage repayments are often still relatively affordable. And that's exactly what has pushed prices up: our ability to *afford* higher prices, thanks to lower interest rates making mortgages cheaper.

If we're trying to save and build wealth, our monthly housing costs (rent or mortgage) matter far more than your home's price. That's because your monthly cashflow determines whether you are saving. And your savings rate dictates whether you are building wealth. It doesn't matter if you have debt or not.

(See the book resources page for an in-depth article on this topic.)

And if you prefer not to own a house at all, that's perfectly fine too. We have this cult-like belief in Australia that you can't be wealthy or retire if you don't own property. That's complete nonsense!

You Don't Need to Own a House to Retire Early

As shocking as that statement might sound to our Aussie belief system, it's true. Here's why: If you've decided to be a long-term investor who rents, your investments can simply pay your rent and other living costs.

"But I'll be paying rent forever?" Well, yes. But your investments will be paying you income forever too, and they'll keep growing over time. Plus, people who own a house will be paying off the mortgage for most of their life as well. If you're someone who prefers the benefits of renting, rest assured that you don't need to own property to live wealthy and free.

So, should you rent or buy? There are great arguments on both sides.

Why You Should Buy

- Security. You'll never be forced to move. The mental freedom of owning your home also has a psychological benefit.
- The forced saving of paying off a mortgage helps you build equity.
- You can do whatever you like: decorate, install solar panels, plant gardens, and so on.
- Buying 'locks in' your house price. As your income grows, your mortgage repayments become more affordable, helping you save more.
- Home ownership is treated favourably by the government and tax system. There's no capital gains tax (CGT) when you sell your home, even for a large profit. A home is also not currently included in the 'assets test' for pension/unemployment benefits.
- Easy access to low-cost debt. Banks will lend at low rates using residential property as security. This could be used as an emergency fund/buffer or for investment opportunities.
- Certainty of cashflow. Once your home is paid off, your expenses will be permanently lower.

Why You Should Rent Instead

- Freedom to move at very little cost. Switch locations, move interstate, or pack-up and travel with no major costs compared to owning. Moving house costs tens of thousands of dollars in stamp duty and agent fees alone.

- Flexibility to scale the cost up or down. If your situation changes, you can easily trade your current place up/down in cost when the lease expires. This also means you can experiment with different areas, property types, and lifestyles to see what you like best.
- Your money is working harder. Not owning a house means all your cash can be tucked away in investments which can provide higher returns over time than having savings tied up in a home. Sure, owning saves you on rent, but comes with countless other bills outside the mortgage: council rates, water rates, insurance, strata fees (for units), repairs and maintenance, moving costs, and more.
- Diversify your wealth. Owning a home means having a lot of money tied up in one single asset, in one location. You might prefer to spread your money across lots of different assets.

Summary

We've lived in both rentals and our own property over the years. Our experience with renting has been pretty good. But there are more long-term emotional benefits from owning your own place. This means it's not strictly a financial decision. For as long as I can remember, it's been cheaper to rent than buy in Australia. The truth is, whether it makes financial sense to rent or buy depends on many things: location, property type, price point, interest rates, rental yields, and expected ownership costs. There's no right answer. Buying a home does mean you're on the hook for all those other bills, but overall, the cost may be similar to renting in many places. This means other factors are more important to the decision.

For achieving financial independence, it doesn't really matter whether you buy or rent. What matters is keeping the monthly cost to a reasonable level, so that you can still save and invest. How do you do that?

Don't Pay For Too Much House

Keep your housing costs under control by choosing a property and location which matches your *needs*, not your *desires*. We all know people who have bought their 'dream house' and are now working non-stop to pay for the privilege. No flexibility, no investments, and no freedom. A dream house can easily turn into a nightmare if it traps you in a high-income job you hate.

On top of that, most of us have lots of unused space in our homes. According to the Australian Bureau of Statistics (ABS), 77% of households have at least one spare bedroom, with many having two or more. We could rent out that space or opt for a smaller property to avoid paying for rooms we don't really need. One less bedroom will often save you thousands per year as a renter, and could mean $50,000-$100,000 (or more) off the price as a buyer.

Not Everywhere Is Expensive

There are plenty of locations around Australia, even in capital cities, where property is more affordable.

If living in an expensive area is preventing you from saving, consider moving. Many people move to lower cost regions and experience multiple benefits: financial, mental health, and life satisfaction. Maybe you'll earn less, but all things considered, you can come out way ahead compared to staying in the bigger city.

Sometimes we feel tied to a certain area due to family. I get that. But we must decide whether it's worth it or not. Living further away in a lower cost place might mean we can work less and spend more time visiting family (either right now or by reaching FI faster). Think about creative solutions to get what you want.

Consider the Trade-offs

If you're set on an area, you could make a trade-off between size and location.

What can you compromise on? A better location and a smaller space, or more space for a less ideal spot? Most people are afraid to make these decisions, and as a result, they make no progress and remain stuck on the hamster wheel.

You'll also see suburbs right next to each other which vary in price dramatically. Often for no good reason, other than the perception of one being 'better' than the other. Funnily enough, these 'ugly duckling' suburbs often catch up in price and gentrify over time. Take advantage of this by opting for a well-located area which isn't quite as pricey as neighbouring suburbs.

Get a Great Mortgage Rate

A mortgage rate of 3.3% instead of 3.8% doesn't sound like a big deal. But on a $600,000 mortgage, the interest difference amounts to $3,000 in a year. You can use these savings to pay off your mortgage years earlier, or build your investments faster. Each of these compounds, so the benefit multiplies over time.

It only takes a short visit at the bank, or on the phone – maybe 15 minutes – for a large ongoing benefit. What if your bank won't give you a good rate? Refinance to another lender, or use a mortgage broker to find a better option. By the way, mortgage brokers are typically free to use: they are paid a commission by the lender afterwards for bringing them a new customer. The mortgage market is highly competitive, so take advantage of it!

Some Reminders about Housing Costs

Yes, property is more expensive these days. But on average, our homes are far bigger and better than they used to be. There are also less people living in each dwelling. This means the space per person is through the roof (see what I did there?).

It might be hard to believe, but the floor area of the average Aussie home is the biggest in the world. Even larger than the land of the McMansions, America.

Plus, homes have become much fancier. You've seen homes for sale with the original 1970s kitchen, bathroom, floors, and fittings, right? Look what we have now – pure luxury in comparison!

Maybe it's not exciting to start in a smaller (or older) place than you'd like. But you can always move up the housing ladder later, when you're in a better financial position. The more you try to live like a wealthy person now, the longer it will take to *become* wealthy.

One final point: buying a home is a lifestyle choice, not an investment. Yes, it may grow in value. But don't bank on it. Buy something you will settle into and live in for a long time. And always remember that whether you buy or rent, costs can still blow out either way.

Cars and Transport

Cars can be a huge money pit, but we often shrug this off and say this is out of our control. We need to get places, and a car is often the quickest way. But in truth, there's a little more to it than that.

That's because we often use cars as a status symbol. We've been told that our vehicle is an extension of us. Part of our image. When you're thinking about a car as a status symbol (rather than as a simple mode of transport), it's easy to get sucked into overspending. Instead, see it for what it is, and separate your self-worth from your vehicle.

While everyone enjoys the convenience and freedom associated with driving, there are plenty of ways to keep the costs under control.

Buy with Cash

If you *need* a loan to get a car, you can't afford that car! Buy something cheaper. Or use public transport, Uber, and a bike until you can buy it with cash. This also makes the purchase feel more real. You're handing over a big pile of your own savings for this vehicle, rather than signing up to an automatic monthly payment you don't really think about.

Car loans just compound a bad decision. That $30,000 car ends up costing $50,000 in loan repayments, and by the time you've paid it off it's worth $10,000. Rinse and repeat every few years and you've got the perfect recipe for lighting your money on fire.

Consider Opportunity Cost

Remember our old friend – *opportunity cost* – from the last chapter? This is what we could have done with the money that's tied up in our vehicles. How much is sitting in your driveway right now? $30,000? $70,000?

A family with two $35,000 vehicles has $70,000 tied up in car ownership. Imagine they replace these with two (still nice and reliable) $10,000 vehicles. This frees up $50,000 to invest. In just 10 years, this money grows to around $100,000, or $200,000 in 20 years. Less expensive cars are also cheaper to repair, insure, and replace, creating an increasing snowball of savings over time. Having a smaller, more efficient vehicle will be just as safe, far more economical, and easier to park. You can always hire a large vehicle for rare occasions when it's truly needed.

Driving your Car is the Cheap Part

Most of our car costs have nothing to do with driving. Here's a few rough estimates of the annual costs of owning a small-to-medium $10,000 vehicle. (Assuming we own it for 10 years and replace it when it goes to car-heaven).

- Yearly registration: $800.
- Insurance (third party): $400.
- Car replacement/depreciation: $1,000 (assuming replacement after 10 years).
- Servicing/Repairs: $500.

We're almost at $3,000 per year and we haven't even left the house! When you add in petrol, loan repayments, and multiple cars per household, it often blows out to 5 times this amount or more. This means we *really* want to question owning a car in the first place.

It's also worth mentioning the mental trap of thinking that just because we already own a car, we should 'get our money's worth' and drive it everywhere. Don't make this mistake! Along with the fixed costs above, every kilometre we drive also burns money due to fuel expenses plus wear and tear. Make no mistake, driving less will have an immediate and direct effect on your car costs.

Re-Thinking Convenience

We tend to think of driving as convenient. But isn't true convenience when we don't have to drive at all? When everything we need most (work, shops, recreation, family, friends) are all nearby?

Commuting to work is a huge burden on our time and wallet. We might need to rethink where we live to find the optimal solution. It's worth spending more on housing to live in a location that's closer to work, more central, or with better public transport. With thoughtful planning, many families can drop their second car, and some people can go car-free!

A lifestyle where you barely need to drive is also more enjoyable. You feel more connected to your local area, and it removes the frustrations of traffic, shitty drivers, and prolonged sitting.

At the very least, a couple should ensure that one spouse's work is nearby, to reduce the need for two cars. This alone will save thousands per year. Here's some more ideas for optimising your car costs:

Drive less often and combine trips.

It's crazy how many people go to the shops nearly every day. Plan your meals and shopping in advance and do it all in one trip per week. This saves time and reduces unnecessary car use. Can you combine errands or delay trips to be more efficient? Driving is a habit, so stop and think about possible alternatives before you assume every car trip is essential.

Do local activities in your spare time.

The weekend is great for getting out and enjoying some freedom. But that doesn't mean we need to grab the car keys. Find ways to enjoy your local area: go for walks, play at the park, meet a friend at the coffee shop, exercise, read a book, or work on your hobbies. If your local area has nothing good to do, maybe reconsider why you live there!

Food

First, let's tackle a big myth: eating healthy does not sentence you to a $300 per week grocery bill. Nor does saving money in this area mean sacrificing health. Well, unless your afternoon treat is a packet of $27 gluten-free organic kale chips, cooked in single origin lime leaf oil that was hand-picked by angels, carefully infused with the joy of a baby's laughter, and lovingly peppered with magical leprechaun dust.

Look, some healthy food is expensive. But not all. And while we're on this topic, avoid falling for the 'superfood' marketing hype. We seem to have this urge for new, magical products that will make us healthy, attractive, trendy and live forever all at the same time (the novelty trap in action). Spend your money on real, whole foods that are just as nutritious, only slightly less exciting because we know about them already!

Cooking and Planning

I'll assume you know that cooking your own food is 2,837 times cheaper than getting takeaway. So, if we're in the 'Making Our Own Food Club', we're essentially getting paid to be our own chef. This leads to healthier habits and the important lifelong skill of looking after ourselves.

To do this, you need a rough idea of what you'll eat during the week, so you can shop effectively. Experiment, and list your favourite dishes and healthy snacks which you can rotate through. When you want to switch it up, or optimise further, Google for alternatives and new recipe ideas.

When you plan what to eat, you make better choices for the whole week, with just a little effort upfront. It's cheaper, healthier, and more emotionally satisfying.

If you're young and cooking your own food seems intimidating, just start with the simplest food you enjoy and go from there. You can always fancy it up later once you develop the habit of cooking simple meals. As a young man, I was certainly no star in the kitchen, but I learned to make tasty and nutritious low-cost meals without much trouble.

Shopping

One powerful shopping habit to optimise your food costs is to look at what things cost 'per kilo', 'per 100g', and 'per litre'. Look for these tiny numbers on the price tags. Rather than searching for the lowest sticker price, look for the best value. That's the difference between cheapskate and frugal.

The frugal shopper will gladly spend more today if it saves more over the long term.

Using this metric helps you maximise your nutrition per dollar. There are plenty of healthy low cost 'per kilo' foods (especially veggies and legumes) that can be combined into highly nutritious meals. Start using this trick and you'll save a small fortune.

Do the Switcheroo

In the last ten years, store-branded products have greatly increased in quality. It's now difficult to tell the difference between store-brand and name-brand. Plus, the likes of Coles and Woolies will refund any of their products that you're not happy with. These are well worth trying as the savings here are huge. And, quite often, the name-brand and store-branded stuff is made in the very same factory!

You can also switch to foods that are similar yet offer better value. Things like frozen berries instead of fresh, peanuts in place of pistachios, lower priced meats, or bananas and oranges instead of mangoes and grapes.

I've found frozen fruit and veg to be just as good (if not better) than the fresh stuff. Typically, it's frozen at a stage of freshness, whereas the store stuff might be a bit old. It's surprisingly easy to swap ingredients in meals to get similar nutrition and taste at a much lower cost. Even if you only do this half the time, the savings will still pile up.

More Veg, Less Meat

This might be contentious, since some people refuse to alter their eating habits. I used to be a heavy meat-eater myself. But I ended up reducing, and then removing, meat and other animal products from my diet entirely (for ethical reasons). After gradually focusing on other foods instead, I feel better and have more energy. But what really surprised me was how our grocery bill started melting away. This switch reduced our weekly food spend by 40%. In short, focusing more on plant-based foods is better for the planet, your wallet, animals, and your health.

Try going meat-free for one meal a week, then one day per week, and see how you go. Like me, you might find that you feel great and it's easier than you expect.

Specials

You already know it's smart to buy more of something when it's on sale. But this is something we can take to the next level. Specials tend to be predictable. For example, you may notice the same thing goes on sale every 4-6 weeks. So here's a good rule of thumb: stock up with enough to last you *at least* until the next time the item goes on special. Don't be shy, fill your cupboards, freezer, and maybe even that spare room you don't use. Yeah, I'm that guy!

Holidays and Travel

Most Aussies tend to spend a fair bit on holidays. It's not hard to spend $20,000 per year on luxurious overseas trips. You might even consider this an essential part of life. But after 20 years this habit will cost you over $800,000 in foregone wealth compared to investing. Is this trade-off worthwhile? International travel is a relatively new concept. Just a couple of generations ago, people almost never travelled overseas. For most of human existence, we simply explored places that were nearby.

This seems unthinkable today, but it's true. Flying for the masses has only been a thing for the last 50-70 years. And I'm talking about rich countries like Australia, because many global citizens still can't afford regular overseas travel. So how do we balance our goal of financial independence with the desire to enjoy holidays and explore new places?

Appreciate Australia

Firstly, we can travel locally, visiting the truly beautiful places in our own country, which, ironically, people from all over the world come to see!

It's easy to under-appreciate what's in our backyard because it seems normal to us. But we have amazing beaches, beautiful forests, and fascinating wildlife. You'll often find that road trips, camping, and exploring is just as stimulating (if not more) than hotels and fancy tours.

You could even rent pet-friendly accommodation and take your dog along. That's what we've done for years, and it's fantastic!

Take Time off at Home for a Taste of FI

Use some annual leave for a taste of early retirement. Whether it's a few weeks or a few days at a time, this creates more freedom immediately, without higher spending.

I did this towards the end of my journey and highly recommend it. Having more days off each month was amazing.

This lets you recharge your batteries, take better care of yourself, and catch up on things you've been meaning to do. When you go back to work, you'll be genuinely refreshed. Sometimes travel itself can be tiring and you don't feel like you got to properly unwind.

Rotate between Experiences

Even if you continue travelling overseas, you can still have a good savings rate. The secret is simply spreading those trips out more. Instead of an overseas trip every year, do it every 2 or 3 years. Or, take turns between local holidays, time off at home, and international travel.

This massively lowers your holiday spending (and your carbon footprint), while also getting the benefits of every option: more free time now, enjoying the beautiful country we live in, and occasionally visiting other cool places too!

Does This Really Make a Difference?

Let's assume a household spends $10,000 per year on overseas holidays. Here's an alternative approach: over three years they take one overseas trip costing $10,000, two nice local trips costing $2,500 each, and use their remaining annual leave for extra days or weeks off at their leisure.

Now their total spend over three years is $15,000 instead of $30,000. That's a massive 50% saving for a relatively small tweak. And they're hardly missing out. They've simply modified their holidays and travel to have greater variety and more quality free time. Strategies like this are how it's possible to save half your income (or more) without any extreme level of sacrifice.

Experience and Meaning

Let's be honest. Some people use travel as an escape from everyday life. A reward for working hard. But would you prefer your life to be amazing for a few weeks of the year, or would you like a genuinely enjoyable life every single day?

I'm not saying you can't have both. But the one we experience more often (our day-to-day experience) deserves greater attention. When you can wake up and have control over every minute of your time, you see holidays for the novelty they are.

The daily experience of freedom is better than any holiday you can go on. It's something you don't want to escape from.

I focus my energy and attention on where I spend the bulk of my existence: everyday life. Any additional positive experiences are a bonus on top of the enjoyment I get from each day. Travel is another perk of affluence that we've become accustomed to.

To be clear, we also went on some lovely overseas trips during our FI journey, including to Africa, Singapore, and Bali. As with most things, do it in moderation. These days, we tend to travel locally so we can take our dog with us. And even though seeing other countries is nice, I'm honestly happier enjoying each day as it comes. Would you rather a few weeks of freedom now, or freedom for the rest of your life?

Longer Term Travel Goals

Another option is to save travelling for later. What if we choose to view travel as a lifelong goal instead of an immediate and fixed part of our annual spending? This way, we're not forgoing travel, simply changing when we do it.

Travel can be a great experience. But these events are short-lived, the holiday-high wears off, and our memories quickly fade. Then we're looking towards the next exciting trip. Doesn't this sound eerily familiar to our relationship with shopping?

If travel is a huge passion for you, consider taking lower cost trips while you build your investments. When you're wealthier, you'll have more time and control over how, when, and where you travel. Not only that, but you won't sacrifice years of your life for the privilege. You can take your time, engage in 'slow travel', and really enjoy the experience.

Insurance

Insurance is a sticky topic, with no right answer for everyone. We each have different circumstances, varying levels of wealth, liabilities, dependents, comfort levels, and risk tolerance. There are extreme positions, like: "always have insurance, you're reckless if you don't", and: "never get insurance, it's a total scam."

As usual, the truth is in the middle. Insurance *is* statistically designed for us to lose, on average, after the insurance company pays for claims, staff, operating costs, advertising, sales commissions, and shareholder profit. So it is rigged against us. But having zero insurance isn't a good idea either, because it can be incredibly useful.

The verdict: only insure things that could cause you real financial damage.

Having said that, peace of mind is valuable, so if you can't stomach the thought of going without certain insurances, I totally understand.

Personally, I tend not to worry about much and instead think about the probabilities of certain events and what I would do in that situation. This means I'm quite selective about insurance and I think hard before signing up. There are too many insurance types to discuss here, but the following is how we can save on insurance while covering against things going wrong.

Have a financial cushion.

As you build up savings and investments, this becomes a growing pool of money you can access in an emergency. Savings are a form of insurance, and the first pillar of your financial strength. This allows you to get rid of what I call 'small problem' insurance: things like 'extras' insurance, warranties for your phone and appliances, and even contents insurance in many cases.

Remember, any money you're not spending on insurance premiums can be invested to grow over time. Then if you ever need that money to pay for something, it's there. So, rather than *paying out* an increasing amount every year for insurance, you'll be *growing* a big pile of investments, which can pay for something if the need arises.

Obviously, for 'big problem' items like a house burning down, or your car smashing into a Maserati, you'll want to keep those insurance policies.

Shop around.

Sadly, insurers often jack up the price every year to customers who stay. It's called the *Loyalty Tax*. The best rates seemingly always go to new customers, so when your renewal comes, shop around and see if you should switch.

Excess.

The excess is the amount you'll have to pay in the event of a claim. Go for the highest possible excess you can afford. This will lower your premiums in many cases. Doing this across multiple insurances will add up to many hundreds, or possibly thousands of dollars each year in lower premiums. It's a case where having savings helps you save even more. Pretty cool, right?

General thoughts.

There is insurance for everything these days. If you're not careful, insurance premiums can quickly pile up to consume a big chunk of your income. For this reason, it pays to put the fear aside, and think critically about what insurances are right for your situation.

Think about how you would cope if the risk that you're insuring against happened. Would it really hurt you financially, or would you be okay? This line of thinking may immediately make you realise there's one or two insurances you don't need.

People with no savings need the most insurance, given there's nothing available to help in an emergency. But the stronger your financial position, the better you can cope with life's bumps. This means you can scale down your insurance as your wealth grows, and instead keep compounding your savings for any future unexpected events.

Supercharge Your Savings: Things to Remember

Change can be difficult, and there's a lot of ideas in here to consider. Just tackle one thing at a time. Think of the bigger picture and the benefits of taking action towards your goals. Imagine your future self being proud of the changes and progress you've made.

Remember, we're not trying to create the cheapest life possible. We're trying to create an enjoyable life that allows us to save for the future. It's about getting the benefits of modern life while keeping the cost under control.

Review your lifestyle expenses regularly. Ask yourself, "What adjustments can I make to get a similar (or better) lifestyle for less?"

Feel free to spend more in an area that's important to you, while trimming the fat from elsewhere. For example, we currently live in a house across from a huge reserve. We could live elsewhere, yet choose not to because my partner loves gardening, and I love being near open green space and nature. Fancy clothes, international travel, and new cars aren't important to us, which balances things out.

Your favourite thing might be going out with friends, but maybe you aren't fussy about your housing. So maybe you live in a small apartment and spend more on socialising. This helps you save without sacrificing what's important to you. There's plenty of wiggle room here.

We've now tackled the biggest areas of spending and discussed strategies to get the best bang for your buck. Implementing these ideas will go a long way to supercharging your savings rate, giving you plenty of spare cash to start buying your freedom.

But we're not done yet. Next up, we're going to tackle those sneaky little places where money is leaking from your life, and discuss why it matters more than you think.

6

Next Level Optimisation

"Beware of little expenses. A small leak will sink a great ship." -
Benjamin Franklin

There's a popular line in personal finance to get your big expenses under control and don't worry about the small stuff. This is true to a point. But in practice, this gives people the idea that small expenses don't matter.

If that were true, anyone with the 'big stuff' covered – modest house, sensible car, non-lavish holidays – would see money piling up year after year. But clearly, that's not what happens. Why? Because we spend this surplus cash elsewhere, without even noticing.

Maybe we spend less on a car, but then develop a restaurant habit. We choose a sensible house, but then get hooked on designer clothes and the latest gadgets. Or, more commonly, we don't even know where it goes. Just a little extra across 20 different categories, and bam! No savings.

In this chapter, you'll learn the surprising power of small wins. You may even come to enjoy these as much as your big savings. Because – whether big or small – progress is what keeps you excited as you move towards your wealthy future.

Why Small Savings Are Powerful

Those who don't respect small amounts of money rarely end up with lots of it.

Or, as early retirement legend Mr Money Mustache so accurately said, "A millionaire is made ten bucks at a time." Think of your personal income like a rickety old ship, which is prone to leaks. Our optional expenses represent leaks in our ship.

You've heard the saying "small leaks can sink a big ship." Whether we have 1 big leak, or 10 little leaks, the outcome is the same.

But when people see water rushing in, they seem to think, "Well, this isn't good, clearly we need a bigger boat." These people rush to chase more income (a bigger boat) to make up for the leaks. But it rarely solves the problem. Instead, the solution is to fix those damn leaks!

As I wrote in chapter four:

"For every $10 per week you can trim from your spending ($520 per year), that's $13,000 less you need in investments. So you're essentially $13,000 closer to FI."

Fixing the Leaks

When I was trying to save more, I wrote down every expense I could think of. I went down the list, one by one, and looked for ways to improve each item. Almost every single time, there was a way we could save in each area, even by a little.

Each year, sometimes twice, I went over the list again. And guess what? Every single year, our spending decreased. Our savings rate went from around 35% to over 70%, all while living a lifestyle that was just as enjoyable.

When you want to achieve something, attention to detail matters.

Even a slight amount of waste in each area adds up to a large amount of

waste across your total finances.

Oil tycoon John D. Rockefeller was obsessed with efficiency. Not coincidentally, he became the wealthiest person in the world after building the most dominant company in history:

"Rockefeller was relentless in ferreting out ways to cut costs. During an inspection tour of a Standard Oil plant in New York, he observed a machine that soldered the lids on cans of kerosene destined for export. Upon learning that each lid was sealed with 40 drops of solder, he asked, "Have you ever tried 38?" It turned out that when 38 drops were applied, a small percentage of cans leaked. None leaked with 39, though. "That one drop of solder," said Rockefeller... "saved $2,500 the first year, but the export business kept on increasing after that and doubled, quadrupled - became immensely greater than it was then; and the saving has gone steadily along, one drop on each can, and has amounted since to many hundreds of thousands of dollars."

– From the book 'Titan: The Life of John D. Rockefeller', by Ron Chernow.

Keep in mind, this is the early 1900s, so these savings would equate to millions of dollars in today's terms. Incremental savings are more powerful than they seem, because small amounts compound into huge sums over time.

If you're unsure where your money goes (and you don't have a giant mortgage or car loan), it's probably leaking out in small increments everywhere else. Still, when you're just starting out, it can be hard to get excited by small numbers. If that sounds like you, here's a little mental trick that I found to be helpful.

How to Measure Your Progress

Let's say you have a net worth of $50,000, split between a savings account and some shares. After optimising your expenses, you're saving $2,000 per month. Even if you don't invest this money, after a year you've saved $24,000. And let's say your existing savings earnt you a measly $1,000 for the year. Your net worth is now $75,000, which sounds like slow progress.

But you started the year at $50,000, so your net worth actually increased by a healthy 50%.

Those who are further along will have a tough time growing their wealth by 50% in one year. As time goes on, your investments will get bigger, and your wealth will increase at a slower percentage because of the big numbers.

Say you have $300,000 of investments, earning a return of $20,000 for the year, while you manage to save $25,000. Your net worth is now $345,000, a 15% increase. Still excellent, but not the same as in the beginning.

You will never grow your wealth at a faster percentage than you can in the early years. That's because the small base means your progress is driven mostly by savings.

Growing your wealth by 50-100% per year is exciting to think about. And it's motivating as a beginner, which is when you need positive feedback the most.

By measuring our results like this, you can capture the truly great progress you're making. This is the magic of starting small, so enjoy it while it lasts! And of course, experienced savers and investors console themselves with the fact that the amounts of money they're dealing with are much larger and compounding is starting to work its magic.

Cafes, Restaurants, & Takeaway

As we feel increasingly time-poor (and because we have more money), this area has become a bigger part of our spending. Dining out and social-related food spending is inevitable and fun. Meeting friends for coffee or lunch. Going on a date with a special someone. Getting some takeaway on the weekend to have a break from cooking.

Reducing this category to zero is not the goal. But because this stuff quickly adds up, my advice is to simply build good habits. A daily latte and sushi for lunch seems like nothing. And it's true, $15 is basically nothing. But when it's every day, it turns into a $4,000 per year habit. Plus, because it's become a daily habit, we're simply running on automatic. We don't get the same level of joy each time because it becomes routine.

However, when we save most of our cafe and restaurant visits for social events and special occasions, we enjoy it much more, while also saving a shit-ton of money in the process.

A little thoughtfulness helps too. We can have an equally good catch up with a mate over $5 coffee as we can over lunch and drinks costing $60.

This could be one of the areas you put a limit on. Once the 'cafe budget' is empty, that's it until next month. Start the allowance at your normal spending level and reduce it slowly over time, to improve your habits, health, and savings. With incremental changes, the difference will be so small, you won't even notice.

I love going out for burgers or a burrito (the meat-free kind, of course). But the taste of freedom is better than anything you can eat at a cafe or restaurant.

Health and Fitness

A healthy lifestyle doesn't have to be expensive. We can achieve incredible health and fitness by spending no more than we do now. Here's a few ideas:

Avoid the fancy health club

Some of these places cost thousands per year and include facilities you'll never use. I get that some people need the gym environment as a motivator. If that's you, and you're a serious gym user, then by all means find a reasonably priced local gym and go for it! Your cost vs benefit will make it worthwhile. For more casual exercisers, however, you're probably better off with the following options.

DIY fitness

You can buy equipment and create your very own home gym. Often, you'll find excellent second-hand equipment online: things like kettlebells, dumbbells, and resistance bands. These last forever and you can easily create full-body workouts with them. We cancelled our gym memberships and bought a home weights setup over 10 years ago (including a squat rack and bench) and never looked back. It saves time, removes driving and the pain of overcrowded gyms, plus we can use it anytime we want.

Maybe you don't even need weights

Your health plan might involve riding your bike everywhere, brisk walks, pushups, pullups, bodyweight squats, sit ups, swimming, and all sorts of incidental exercise like yard work, home maintenance, and playing with your kids/dog. You can build an attractive physique without lifting heavy weights.

Gear and nutrition

For some reason, when people start focusing on their fitness, they also add $500 worth of clothes and a cupboard full of supplements to the yearly bill. Care to guess why? Clever marketing. But both are unnecessary if you already have comfortable clothes and healthy food at home. Living an active and healthy life isn't complicated. Eat nutritious food, get outside for some sunshine, and spend time actively using your body each day.

Smartphones

These are basically a staple of modern life. They are incredibly useful, yet can easily hoover up all your time and attention. Most people have room to cut the fat in this area without losing any benefits.

The new phone trap

It's mind blowing the amount of people signing up to get a new phone, while locking themselves into a multi-thousand-dollar contract! You know, where the phone is somehow 'free'?

Sidestep this bonanza of insanity by *using your savings* to buy a new phone outright. Better yet, get a good quality second-hand smartphone. And no, you don't need the new iPhone 32, or whatever number we're up to by the time you're reading this. The recent models have 99% of the same features and capability as the brand-new ones.

The best deals

When you buy a phone outright, you're now in a position of power. You get to choose the best prepaid deals from any provider you like. Thanks to fierce competition, costs have fallen massively in the last 10 years, with great deals available for less than $20 per month.

I've found that the 365-day expiry plans are excellent value for money. I've been using these for years at an average cost of $10 per month. Many people pay 5-10x that amount on their phone plan.

A quick google search and you'll find plenty of options, with the new telco providers using the same networks as the more expensive plans. If you have broadband at home and WiFi at work, you can probably go for a lower data phone plan than you realise.

Other tips

For most people, the biggest cost in this area is the phone itself. The easiest way to reduce this is to keep your current phone for as long as possible. At the very least, if you currently upgrade your phone every two years, make it every four years. There – you just effortlessly cut the cost by 50%!

Oh, and get a phone cover! It irritates me to see the amount of people who don't do this. They drop their phone once and the screen becomes a web of cracks. Oh well, time for a new phone! Maybe, subconsciously, that's the plan? Get a good cover that opens and closes – problem solved.

Utilities

Another sneaky area where cash leaks out of our ship is utilities like power and gas. The amount spent can vary dramatically depending on your setup and habits. Here's a few thoughts to power up your savings:

Shop around for power and gas deals

Are you sensing a theme? Look up what deals different energy providers are offering in your state. You might want to check out the government website *Energy Made Easy* to compare local providers. And deals change regularly, so you'll want to check at least once a year.

Pay more for energy efficient appliances and lights

Extra spent here will typically save you more money over time, especially when it comes to big power-suckers like fridges. You might spend a few hundred extra, but the energy savings can be multiples of that over time. Another easy win is to switch your home lights over to LEDs if you haven't already.

Solar panels

Consider getting solar panels if you're a homeowner. From people I've spoken to, it's one of the best decisions they've made. And given Australia is one of the sunniest countries in the world, you'll generally get a high return on investment. Plus, improving technology is making solar panels cheaper and more efficient every year.

Minimise usage

Rug up in winter with more clothes, slippers, and blankets rather than switching on the heating. It's cosier, reduces your environmental footprint, and saves cash. In summer, use ceiling and portable fans rather than turning on the air-con. Instead of blasting the AC all year round out of habit, be mindful of your usage and you'll become surprisingly adaptable to changes in weather. Toughen up a little!

Optimisation Day

It's possible to nail down big savings on your current bills in a short space of time. Your 'per hour' earnings for doing this are often incredible. Even better, you can get most of this done in a day. You might like to turn this into an annual event called *Optimisation Day*.

This is where you calmly take a freshly sharpened blade to your ongoing bills. Things like your mortgage, insurances, phone, internet, and utilities.

And in case you need any more motivation, here are the benefits:

- **Huge savings.** Shaving $2,000 per year off a few expenses (and investing these savings) will compound to $25,000 in ten years, and $66,000 in twenty years.
- **Lower expenses mean you need less to retire.** Having $2,000 less bills means you need $50,000 less to reach FI. A dollar saved is equivalent to twenty-five dollars earned.
- **Bring your freedom forward.** Due to the heavenly combination above – building wealth faster while needing less – you can retire earlier.
- **Avoid the loyalty tax, AKA the lazy tax.** Instead of getting shafted for loyalty, make sure you're getting looked after or take your business elsewhere.
- **Pay off your home sooner.** A lower interest rate means more cash for investing or becoming debt-free faster, saving thousands in unnecessary interest costs.
- **Psychological benefits.** You'll get a happiness boost from feeling more empowered and knowing you're in total control of your finances. Lower bills and lower stress go hand in hand.

You might even like to take a day off work to do this. For employees, you're now *getting paid* to sit around and save money! Less cash going out is just as good (if not better) as more cash coming in. Essentially, you're giving yourself a pay rise.

But even if you don't nail down any extra savings, the action itself gives you confidence that you're on top of things. And because of that, feel free to treat yourself to your favourite food and a special beverage as you bask in the glorious accomplishment of a job well done.

"I have kids, can I still retire early?"

Yes! The FI community is filled with people with different circumstances. Sure, kids aren't without costs. But they don't magically blow up your finances like some claim. Like every other area of spending, it depends on our personal choices. And while I don't have kids myself, countless parents have reached out to confirm this is true.

Here's a few tips for dealing with kids and saving for FI at the same time:

Childcare

Often pointed to as a monstrous hurdle for families trying to save. Fortunately, the Aussie government covers a fair chunk of this cost (often 50% or more), for families on incomes of $250,000 or less. You may have less income after costs than a childless couple, but you probably chose to have children for non-financial reasons, right?

Housing

As it turns out, a small human doesn't take up that much space. The trap is thinking every small child needs their own room, a backyard, plus you need a spare room, and plenty of space for all the extra stuff. Before you know it, you've got an oversized house and you're wondering how the hell you became strapped in this hamster wheel where you're effectively working for the bank. My advice? Minimise the space you need. Have young kids share a room, which will also teach them about compromise and being considerate.

Toys

Kids don't need as many toys as you think. Ever notice that young kids are just as happy playing in a huge cardboard box as they are with the toy that came inside? They don't know how much things cost. Their imagination enables them to create fun out of whatever is around them.

Clothes

Because kids outgrow things so fast, avoid buying new clothes where you can. Check out Gumtree or Facebook marketplace to find good quality second-hand items. Hell, you'll find that many people (including your friends) are happy to simply give away stuff their kids have outgrown. Now, sure, teenagers are a different story. But this is when you'd start to sprinkle in important values and life lessons, like working for what they want rather than just expecting to receive things.

Other thoughts

Kids need their parents more than they need stuff. They need love, time, and attention more than they need a new iPad or a house deposit in 20 years. I know that might seem easy for the guy with no kids to say. But if I had kids,

I would be ruthlessly frugal to create more freedom to spend as much time with them as possible.

(For more on achieving FI with kids, you'll find a great article by a reader of my blog on the book resources page. He shares some excellent tips which I wholeheartedly endorse).

Speaking of kids, most people are concerned about climate change for this very reason: the world we're creating for future generations.

Saving the Planet and Building Wealth

Roughly 100% of people reading this book live on a tiny blue speck we call Earth. Until Elon Musk helps us set up camp on other planets, it's kind of important how things turn out for this rotating mass we call home.

Even if you're a narcissistic sociopath who doesn't care about the environment, you probably still care about your own wealth. Luckily, many of the choices we make that are better for the planet also help us maximise our savings. Here's a few examples.

Where We Live

The more space each human consumes, the less that's left for nature. You don't need to cram 5 kids and 3 dogs into a studio apartment, but being mindful of our 'per-person' footprint helps. We could choose to take up less land, optimise our living space, or rent out extra rooms for maximum efficiency. In return, we benefit from lower mortgage repayments or rent, lower council rates, and smaller power bills. It also means less resources are needed to build, repair, and improve each home over time.

How We Get Around

Our favourite mode of transport (large cars mostly carrying one person) are currently a major polluter and a savings sinkhole. To combat this, we could choose a smaller, more fuel-efficient vehicle.

We can also minimise driving by walking or biking instead, living in a more convenient location, using public transport, and doing more local activities.

What We Fuel Ourselves With

Given that half of Earth's habitable land is used for agriculture (mostly meat and dairy), our eating habits also have a large impact on the planet.

Land clearing for cattle grazing is causing the loss of habitat for countless animals and insects, which is sad because it's becoming clear that humans can live perfectly healthy lives without eating meat. In fact, research suggests a more plant-based diet will lead to a longer, healthier life.

You could also consider eating more locally grown food, to minimise the transport involved. And of course, takeaway food always seems to include a ridiculous amount of packaging, wrappers, and bags.

Free Time

We can even make more Earth-friendly choices about how we spend our spare time. Things like hanging out with family and friends, enjoying our parks and beaches, exercising and being active, working on our hobbies, creating or fixing things, volunteering in the community, or helping others.

But if we decide we can only enjoy our free time by travelling around the world and buying shit, that will be a destructive and ultimately less fulfilling strategy. One is high cost, with poor side effects. The other is low cost, and much richer in rewards.

(If you need some ideas, I wrote an article titled "50 enjoyable low-cost things to do", which you can find on the book resources page.)

Clothing and Gadgets

Unless you're a nudist, you've probably accumulated a wardrobe full of clothing to stay warm and comfortable year-round. Clothing which we rotate through and eventually replace. But somehow this activity of updating our stuff has turned into a game for many people.

Each year we toss out the old and get a fresh consumer high by buying new items. This also happens with technology, appliances, basically everything. Novelty never ends, remember?

Not only does this create an atrocious amount of landfill, but making these items also creates pollution and consumes resources. So, what can we do about it?

The most effective strategy is to simply get your entertainment elsewhere (see above). Next, aim to keep your current stuff longer. Essentially, I'm telling you to do nothing, just keep your stuff. It couldn't possibly be easier! And when things do need to be replaced, consider good quality second-hand items where feasible.

Buying Green

I love the idea of 'green' products: things which are produced sustainably, using recycled materials, or items that are generally more efficient and less wasteful. But this has turned into a bit of a marketing gimmick (as with anything that gains popularity). The never ending conveyor belt of bullshit that is the advertising industry is now pushing us to replace what we currently have with 'greener' options.

While this sounds all sweet and innocent, it creates a problem. If we don't need to replace what we have, then we're doing more harm than good, because buying green products is more destructive than buying no products. Almost always, the best approach for the planet and for your wealth is to not buy things unless you truly need them.

The 'Why' Behind Frugality

No matter our motivation for pursuing financial independence, keeping the Earth in mind is a strong reason to embrace frugality. When we approach our lifestyle and spending decisions like this, it comes from a place of love, not only for the next generation of humans, but also for all the other creatures we share this planet with. As humans, we seem to think we're easily the most important species. But consider this: if we disappeared tomorrow, plants and animals would flourish. Yet, if all the plants and animals disappeared, we wouldn't last long at all.

Frugality, then, is all about thoughtfully considering the true impact of our decisions.

It's not about living like a poor person. Over-generalising, poor people are typically struggling to get by. They spend all their income, buy on impulse, juggle debt repayments, feel trapped by their situation, and live week to week.

On the other hand, a wealthy person feels in control. They have plenty of cash and investments. They've built strong financial habits and make long term decisions.

Consider someone following the advice in this book. Overwhelmingly, they resemble the wealthy person we just described. Remember, the point is not to live a life of sacrifice. It's to live a *better* life.

While that can mean less 'treats' in the short term, it comes with more freedom and meaning over the long term. Besides, you can always spend a little more as your wealth grows anyway.

Winning the Lotto

What many people point to as 'the good life' is just consumerism on steroids: a materialistic, desperate pursuit of one short-term high after another. But I propose that *we're already living the good life.* It's just that nobody bothers to stop and notice.

We're living at the richest time in human history. Fact. In one of the most prosperous countries in the world. Fact. With record levels of personal wealth, material luxury, and the highest ever living standards. Fact. We're living longer and healthier lives than ever. Fact.

Not convinced? How would you like to trade places with someone in rural Africa? What about living back in the early or even mid 1900s? What, doesn't sound so good? Well, there's your answer.

Our perception of 'the good life' is completely skewed by the tiny fraction of the world around us. We fail to put into context how other people live globally and everyone who's lived before us. Much of the world could rightly think of us as extremely spoiled and entitled if they knew we regarded a simple life in modern-day Australia as anything less than heaven on Earth. Yet, despite being among the luckiest and wealthiest people in the world, we *still* look at those just above us and think we're somehow missing out. This is a wildly inaccurate and ungrateful perspective. If we're going to measure ourselves against others, it should be against the other 99.99% of human life that has existed.

Balancing Your Desires and Savings

I'm not advocating deprivation. So, if you begin wishing the days away on your FI journey, something is off. Maybe you need to revisit your values and make more room in your life (and budget) for what's important to you.

For example, maybe you're saving half your income, but it seems restrictive. Feel free to allocate extra cash to where you think it will bring the most fulfilment, whether it's socialising, travel, or something else.

If you notice yourself wishing time would speed up, understand that's a totally normal feeling. Like with any big goal, it's natural to become impatient.

But we really don't want to skip ahead to the future for (at least) two reasons:

1. All the time we have on this earth is valuable. There'll likely come a point where we would give anything to have more time. Keep this at the front of your mind and find ways to appreciate each day while you work towards your goals.
2. As you go through this journey, you're becoming a different person. One who is learning, growing, and expanding your life options. If you snap your fingers and wake up financially free, you miss out on all the personal growth, experience, and accomplishment along the way.

   "In the end, it is the person you become, not the things you have achieved, that is the most important." - *Les Brown*

Rather than just waking up with wealth, the real value lies in becoming the person who has created wealth and achieved a huge goal. You get to keep that feeling forever, and it fuels all your future endeavours too.

Of course, you can also consider options like semi-FI to bring as many of your retirement plans as possible into your current lifestyle. Keep in mind, sometimes just changing jobs or picking up a new hobby is all we need to bring that sense of enjoyment back to our lives, which can keep us going while we work towards our ultimate goal.

At the end of the day, we get to enjoy the best parts of life that everyone else does. The biggest benefit of being rich is not luxuries. It's freedom. And for those who adopt the principles in this book, that can be created surprisingly quickly.

Splurges and the Illusion of Missing Out

There's nothing wrong with the odd splurge. That's because – if we're sensible most of the time – we'll make huge financial progress without the need for silly restrictions or guilty feelings. This is the Art of Moderation.

Of course, a smartarse is quick to suggest that we can enjoy yachts, Maseratis, and Gucci bags in moderation, too. But this isn't about enjoying *everything* in moderation. It's about enjoying *what matters* in moderation. Once we decide what's truly important to us, we can go ahead and enjoy those things in a healthy amount.

This attitude will give you a sense of calm knowing that you're losing nothing. Yet at the same time, you're gaining so much, because of your inevitable financial independence. We each get to design our own adventure. So, to put it bluntly, if the FI journey is making you miserable, you're doing it wrong!

Perception and Judgement

Sometimes people are hesitant to make spending or lifestyle changes because they're worried how others will perceive them. The problem is, we judge others on weak and superficial things, like what we can see and hear.

People with expensive things are perceived as rich. We see the stuff, but we don't see their bank account. We can't see if they have debt. We don't know whether they have any investments. The important information is invisible. We're only seeing what they're choosing to show us, which is easy to fake.

In this way, what we see is misleading. Most importantly, worrying about how other people perceive us is a recipe for disaster, anxiety, and misery. We can't control what people think, and it's not healthy to focus on things we can't control.

> "Care about what other people think and you will always be their prisoner." - *Lao Tzu*

Final Thoughts on Optimising Your Spending

Sometimes people think spending more is a reward. But increasing your spending is more like a burden, because you've just increased your required income and created a new baseline for what you think you need to be happy.

Everyone spends money to treat themselves. That's fine. But the ultimate way to treat yourself is by gaining control over your life. The sooner we realise that a 'good life' is not measured by our yearly spending, the better off we'll be.

Until you're financially independent, each expense should be weighed against an alternate purchase: freedom. Is it still worth it? Lots of stuff is, but many things are not!

I hope this chapter helped see how lots of seemingly small wins can have a multiplier effect on your progress. A little bit at a time, your savings rate will keep climbing until it reaches a comfortable balance of enjoyment, efficiency, and alignment with your goals and values.

You may even choose to implement all these savings strategies to their fullest, add more of your own ideas, and take the fast lane to financial independence. But we don't need to wait until we're FI to build a more satisfying life. We can start right now, by appreciating life's little details and enjoying the small things each day.

A nice walk at sunset. Laughing with a friend. Listening to birds chirping and watching them go about their day. Taking time to notice and feel grateful for these things – literally smelling the roses – genuinely makes you happier. Slow down and appreciate what you already have.

Next up, we're talking about how you can earn more money, along with some important skills, traits, and mindset tips that will help you on your journey.

7

Income, Skills, and Mindset

"Do the best you can, and don't take life too serious." - *Will Rogers*

We've talked a lot about optimising our expenses. But that's only one side of the ledger. Having more money coming in is just as helpful as having less going out. And once you've mastered the art of not spending all your income, earning more can really juice your results.

On the road to FI, I made a conscious effort to increase my income. This helped us grow our investments aggressively and build wealth faster. If you want to bring more cash into your life, here are 10 strategies for boosting your bottom line:

Strategy 1: Work More Hours

Earning extra money by working additional hours isn't the sexiest idea. Nor is it the most creative. But it works!

I put in a fair bit of overtime at my warehouse job over the years. While it wasn't exciting, working extra hours provided a big boost to my income.

Thanks to penalty rates, the higher wage you earn for overtime means your *average hourly rate* can be higher, which makes it an incredibly simple and effective way to boost your annual earnings.

Strategy 2: Work Different Hours

In addition to that, depending on your job, working *different* hours can also grow your income. As a naive teenage worker, I couldn't fathom why anyone would volunteer to work afternoon or night shifts. Later, it became clear that the pay was higher for afternoon and night work – sometimes much higher. Wow, sign me up!

Considering that I was doing exactly the same job, this felt like a no-brainer. Working different hours *and* extra hours helped me turn a $55,000 per year job into one where I often earned $85,000 (my highest year was $97,800). If you can work shifts or weekends, consider switching up your work hours to boost your paycheck.

Now, this won't be possible for everyone. Those in traditional salaried jobs which don't pay overtime will need to look at other ways to increase their income.

Strategy 3: Switch Employers

Not every employer pays the same for a given job role. The difference in pay for the same job can be tens of thousands per year. So if you're looking to boost your income, this is one of the best methods. See what other employers are offering for your specific role, using sites like Indeed and Seek. How do the pay and conditions compare?

Instead of shopping around for the best deal on your bills, you're shopping around for the best employer. My partner increased her yearly income by over $15,000 by switching employers. Not only was the pay better, but the work environment was nicer, and the workload was less.

Part of this is recognising your own value. Plenty of people spend only a couple of years at each employer and get a variety of skills, projects, and connections under their belt. Then, they use this to leverage their way into higher paying positions. If you're struggling for ideas, entry level government positions pay quite well, and there's good opportunity for advancement.

Strategy 4: Switch Roles

Get curious and think about your 'big picture' skills rather than what's specific to your current job. Things like problem solving, communication, attention to detail, organising, and so on. What traits and abilities do you have that can apply to other roles?

Depending on where you work, there may be other jobs you'd be well suited for within the same organisation. If management knows you're interested in a change, they may even help find you something, rather than risk losing a good employee. Otherwise, consider putting your hand up to help in other areas when they need someone to fill in. This can help you learn about other well-paying roles that you could slot into in the future.

And remember, if you don't like the new position, you can always go back to your old line of work. This strategy is all upside, no downside.

Strategy 5: Switch Industries

Sometimes it's worth looking around to see what people with similar roles and skill sets are earning in different industries. Do any of these jobs sound appealing?

Let's say you're a Courier Driver. It's not a stretch to think that with some extra training, you could be driving vehicles in the mining industry. Difference in pay? Massive.

Or maybe you work in retail. You're good with people but retail isn't paying well. You could easily get started in sales and see how you like it. There are similar skills involved, but sales has enormous upside potential if you're good.

There are plenty of ways you can do similar work for a vastly increased income, simply by moving to a different industry or sector.

Strategy 6: Climb the Ladder

This is a classic, time-tested strategy for increasing your income.

Maybe you ask to take on more responsibility and deliver on your promise, proving your capability. When a higher role becomes available, you'll be one of the first people that comes to mind.

Alternatively, you could opt for further study and training to enhance your knowledge, and get a higher paying job that way. If you know your current job well, offer to train new employees, or help out when the supervisor is away.

There are lots of little ways you can show you're ready and willing to move up the ranks.

Strategy 7: Negotiate a Raise

It's not enough to approach your employer and say, "I've been working hard, I deserve a raise."

While this might be true, it's not very strategic. Unless you can prove you're worth more, you're basically just asking for a handout. But let's say you come up with specific ideas and create efficiencies in the workplace which either makes or saves the company money. Now you have some leverage.

Any sensible employer will reward an employee who can come up with revenue-boosting or cost-cutting strategies. Another idea is to work your arse off and show your boss how valuable you are. Later, you can negotiate a pay-rise based on your increased performance.

If you genuinely become a more valuable employee, it's only fair that you're compensated for it. And if your current employer isn't willing to pay up, find an employer who will reward your hard work and initiative.

Strategy 8: Side Hustles

A side hustle is all about using your spare time to earn extra cash. This might involve a second job, or even a little micro-business, which is more possible than ever thanks to freelance sites like Airtasker, Fiverr, and others.

There's a million ways you can make extra money in your spare time: cleaning homes, pet sitting, selling plants, building things, teaching, buying and fixing items to re-sell, online freelance work, or something else entirely. The options are endless!

Ideally, pick something you enjoy doing, then it's a win/win hobby!

Strategy 9: The Sharing Economy

Use the sharing economy to rent out things you own. Renting out a room in your home is a big potential earner. According to data from house-share platform Flatmates, the average spare room in Australia is now worth over $10,000 per year, with higher prices achieved for in-demand suburbs close to transport and amenities.

You can even rent out your car, parking spot, any storage space you have, and more.

Of course, be sure to check the tax implications of any new income-earning activity, including what deductions you may be entitled to (the ATO will find you!).

Strategy 10: Sell Stuff You Don't Need

Offloading rarely-used possessions is a great way to make extra cash and reduce clutter. If you wouldn't pay to acquire an item that you currently own, then don't own it! Sell it to create more space, money, and mental freedom.

You might even realise you don't need a home quite so big, and instead downsize or use that space more productively.

Years ago, we sold our second car and bought a scooter, since my partner's work was only a short trip away. The proceeds were invested, and we saved thousands per year on fuel, maintenance, and depreciation. We also recently moved house and managed to sell about $1,300 worth of items we didn't need, including some weights, a spare bed, and a few old phones.

(Bonus Strategy 11: Investing)

That's right. You can start increasing your annual income as soon as you begin investing. At first, it probably won't be much, unless you already have significant savings. But over time, as you build investments, you will receive an increasing amount of passive income from the assets you own.

We'll speak about investing very soon, but I just wanted to throw this one in here to get the idea floating around in your mind. Your investments will become a bigger part of your annual income over time, and any money you add will directly increase the earnings you derive from this area. For example, every $2,500 invested can provide $100 per year in passive income – a growing stream of earnings you can enjoy for the rest of your life.

Adding It Up

Is the extra effort worth it? Well, *just one* of the above ideas could easily boost your annual income by $10,000. Over 15 years, this creates an extra $250,000 of wealth, thanks to investment returns.

And if you stack up more strategies you could comfortably add $20,000 (or even more) to your annual earnings. This would result in $500,000 over 15 years. These are impressive sums, but what impact does this have on our timeframe to early retirement?

A household earning $100,000 and spending $60,000 has a 40% savings rate. By earning $110,000 and spending $60,000, they're now saving 46%. That doesn't sound like much, but their timeframe to retirement falls from 21 years to 18 years. Three extra years of freedom! By earning $120,000, their savings rate moves to 50%. And FI is now achievable in 16.5 years: nearly half a decade faster.

Having said that, be careful you don't catch *side hustle fever.* This is where you're filling every waking minute with a money-making activity so that you can retire earlier. Some extra hustle is healthy and natural when you have a big goal to accomplish (and when you genuinely enjoy whatever you're working on). But you need to strike the right balance between working hard and becoming a slave to chasing money. There's no point going so hardcore that your relationships, physical and mental health start to suffer!

Is It Possible to Achieve FI on a Low Income?

It's absolutely possible to build substantial wealth as a lower income earner. However, there are some key differences:

1. **You have even more to gain by increasing your earnings.** If you boost your income from $40,000 to $50,000, that's a 25% increase. Someone

earning $100,000 needs to increase their income by $25,000 to have the same effect. This gain can flow straight to your savings rate.

2. **You don't have as much room to be sloppy with your spending.** Higher earners can get away with having a few more leaks in their ship than you can. Put another way, you'll need to become a master at prioritising. This means scrutinising each expense more closely: is this really worth it? Am I getting value from this transaction? Can I get the same thing for less?

Fortunately, wages in Australia (even for relatively unskilled positions) are quite healthy compared to other countries. Even a minimum wage full-time worker now has 50% more income after inflation than an equivalent worker in 1980. And while the minimum wage isn't huge, Australia has the highest minimum wage in the world (when all countries are measured on a purchasing power basis).

Better yet, most jobs pay more than minimum wage. Having said that, if you're on the lower end of the income scale, you don't need to stay there! Use the strategies we've covered here and find multiple ways to scale up your income.

(I wrote an article listing over 60 jobs that don't require a degree and pay at least $60,000 per year. See the book resources page.)

Plus, if you're on a low wage right now, you may even have an advantage. Wait, what?

That's right. You're already good at living on a low income. That means when more money starts coming in, nearly all of it can go towards saving and investing. The big income, big spenders often have greater trouble adjusting because of their own embedded spending habits, and it's not as easy for them to continue ratcheting up their income.

How you manage your money is far more important than how much money you manage.

So my advice for lower earners is the same. Look at where your money is going, optimise your expenses, and boost your income. I'm not saying it's going to be easy. But it's still doable.

If you're a low-income family, you may already be spending less hours at work than your peers, especially if you have one stay at home parent. That makes saving tough, but it does mean you're getting precious quality time with your kids which other people aren't. That's a healthy trade-off. Later, when the kids are older, you can increase your income to juice your progress. But right now, as long as you're putting money aside for investing or paying down debt, your situation will improve every year.

What if you're single? Well, it means you can't spread your household costs over two salaries like couples can. But it also means you can make any financial, work, and lifestyle changes more easily, without disrupting the harmony of the household. You can do whatever you like: move locations, work extra hours, ruthlessly cut spending. Maybe you move closer to work and get rid of your car. You could also dramatically reduce your housing costs by renting out a room, or sharing with someone else.

Given our two core strategies for increasing our savings rate – earn more and spend less – you might be wondering which one is more effective.

Earn More or Spend Less?

To state the obvious, both are incredibly helpful. Earning more AND spending less is the one-two punch that really gives your finances that rocket-fuel to take off. But if I'm forced to pick sides, then spending less is *usually* the winner. The first reason is the 25x multiplier benefit of needing less to reach FI due to lower spending.

Secondly, most people don't have an income problem: they have a spending problem. Since most of us earn reasonably good incomes here in modern-day Australia, shooting for more money before improving our spending strikes me as missing the bigger picture. Sure, there's technically no limit on your earnings. But you've only got limited energy to devote to earning, and limited hours in the day.

On the other hand, spending less is a *permanent reduction* in the amount of money you need. That's hugely powerful, and less of a burden to carry throughout life. Our desires on the other hand, can simply increase with our income. The more we feed those desires, the more they grow. Like cancer. We can easily end up on an extremely elegant, gold-plated treadmill...but it's still a treadmill to nowhere.

Here's an example. A doctor earning $500,000 and saving $50,000 per year is in roughly the same position as a labourer earning $50,000 and saving $5,000 per year. Both are saving 10% of their pay, and both can retire at the same time. Sure, the doctor's life is fancier. But in truth, their freedom and happiness is likely to be about the same.

Don't get me wrong, earning more will absolutely make a difference, especially if your income is on the lower end. But we also must put a value on our free time, and avoid succumbing to the 'hustle, hustle' culture of chasing more money and working until your eyes bleed. The mental health toll is rarely worth it.

Work on your expenses first. Then ratchet up that income and plough it all into investments (which we're talking about next!). Getting your spending sorted first will help you use that extra cash wisely when it starts coming in.

Keeping your lifestyle the same as your income grows is the greatest personal finance hack that almost nobody does.

To create an extraordinary result, we can't make the ordinary choices everyone else does. One philosophy that addresses this head-on is Minimalism.

Minimalism: When Less Is More

Minimalism is about removing things that are no longer serving us, so we can focus our time, energy, and money on what matters most. Things that could be deemed unnecessary might include clutter around our house, old bank accounts we don't use, or clothes we never wear. Minimalism also encourages us to question adding new things to our lives until they've been carefully considered first.

But it's more than that. I think of Minimalism as the power of focus, combined with the art of simplifying. Here's why it's useful:

We've been convinced that accumulating possessions is part of a good life and something to celebrate. But aside from the environmental issues, it's bad for our mental health. Clutter makes people anxious and creates sensory overload. On the other hand, a minimalist home with lots of clear and clean space is far more calming and aesthetically pleasing.

When we recently moved house, I was shocked (and slightly ashamed) at the amount of stuff we had. Even for a frugal two-person household, it just seemed like so much! Many items were given away or sold, giving us more space, more cash, and feeling lighter for it. You don't realise how much shit you have until you move. When you relocate every item you own, that's when you begin to resent how many things there are. Simply dealing with it all takes so much time. Quite often, the stuff we own ends up owning us.

And it's not just *stuff.* We've even been convinced to cram as many activities into our limited time as possible, at work and home. When do we get time to really breathe? To relax and decompress? Many people are overwhelmed because they've been told a good life has to be overflowing with things to do. We've become addicted to being busy. Always doing, always striving, always talking, always scrolling. But it's destroying our peace of mind.

Our minds crave simplicity. The less cluttered our schedule, the more freedom we have. The less cluttered our finances, the easier they are to manage. And the less cluttered our mind, the clearer our thoughts.

By simplifying your commitments, this frees up time and energy to make bigger changes in your life. Things may have popped into your mind already. Maybe it's moving house, selling a car, finding a better job, or optimising your other expenses. Give yourself enough space to tackle these important tasks. The status quo may leave you stuck, drowning in activities and obligations, never getting around to any of it.

In short, keeping things simple is better for our sanity, our happiness, and our finances. Minimalism fits perfectly with our goal of financial independence and building a great life.

We don't need to dump our possessions and go live in a cave. We simply need to develop a stronger filter for what's worth caring about. If you're not sure whether something is truly meaningful or not, then it's probably not.

So, how do you know if you've got too much stuff? Well, does the thought of moving house give you shivers? That's a good way to gauge how much 'excess baggage' we've accumulated. Because that's the thing: when we buy a new item we're stuck lugging it around forever.

Dipping your toe into Minimalism can lead to some incredibly cool benefits:

- Higher savings. Questioning what's essential will mean you'll naturally spend less.
- Lower stress. Fewer possessions means less clutter, creating a more relaxing environment.
- More free time. Simplifying your life reduces your obligations, leading to more freedom.
- You can make money selling stuff you barely (or never) use. Win, win!
- Lower housing costs. Less space taken up by possessions gives us the ability to live in a smaller home or rent out the additional space.
- Better for the environment. Anything new we buy has an environmental cost, and old possessions can be donated or recycled.
- Less to clean, organise, maintain, and replace. Our possessions take up more of our time than we think.
- Easier to find things, clean, prepare for visitors, and move house when you need to.
- More energy, space, and money to focus on the most important things

in your life.

- Less is more. Less means more savings, space, time, and tranquillity. Minimalism is not about living a sparse, empty life. It's about learning to pick the most fruitful things and squeeze more juice out of them.

"In a world with infinite information and opportunity, you don't grow by knowing or doing more, you grow by the ability to correctly focus on less" - *Mark Manson*.

As we continue building our mindset in this chapter, I want to share some important traits and skills which help us along our journey.

Characteristics of Happy Achievers

Learn Not to Care What Others Think

Other peoples' opinions will always mean something to you. But you can't let it rule your life. More than anything, you need to feel good about who you are on the inside. Then, whether people think you're a hero or a zero, it won't affect your happiness.

If anything, by taking a different path you'll likely end up with greater respect from others, since it takes bravery to stray from the pack. Measure yourself based on what's important to you, not others. Warren Buffett calls this 'your inner scorecard'.

Look around at the people you work with in their 50s and 60s. Do they look happy? Is that what you want for your life? Probably not. So why the hell would you care if other people think this FI thing is weird?

Focus on the Bigger Picture

It's easy to get bogged down in details. But the big picture is what matters. If you blow a few hundred bucks here and there, or pick a few sub-par investments, it doesn't matter. Just keep saving and investing, and you're bound to become wealthy.

There's no need to agonise over every little thing. If you've got the basics right, cut yourself some slack. Plus, the main goal is not to become mega rich (though that may happen eventually). It's to build a more meaningful existence. Remember the lifestyle you're working towards, not just the number in your bank account.

Take Ultimate Responsibility

Most successful people have a 'no excuses' mindset. They take control of their life and accept responsibility for the good and bad. They don't look at others and point out why they had it easier. Instead, they make the most of their situation and look for ways to make it work, rather than reasons why it won't.

You can't control everything that happens, but it's your job to deal with life as best as you can. When something goes wrong, your default reaction should be: "OK, what can I do about it?" Or: "How can I improve/fix this situation?"

This puts the onus back on us, rather than hoping the universe will magically step in to help. If you can improve or fix something, do it. If you can't, then there's no use worrying about it.

Be Guided by Freedom, Not Fear

People are naturally afraid of running out of money if they quit their job. But you have the knowledge, skills, and potential to earn plenty of extra income later if you need to, or if you decide that your original FI number is not enough. Don't let the fear of 'not having enough' keep you at work when you've already met your goal.

This addiction to safety is a miserable way to live. It will lead you down a path of regret. Unfortunately, it's more common than you might think, and can often be boiled down to fear of the unknown. Complete freedom is intimidating. Meanwhile, staying in a cushy job is comfortable, so our brain plays tricks on us to keep us there. But we ventured down this path for a reason, so remember why you're doing this.

Speaking of fears, there's a big one that's infected our culture in the last 10 years: the fear of missing out (FOMO).

Dealing With FOMO

I see and hear from people in their 20s and 30s struggling to make decisions in their lives and conflicted by options. They want to save, but they want to spend. They want to get married and have kids, but they want to work less and have more free time. They want security, but they want freedom. They want to live in the moment, but they want a great life in 10 years. And they want it all, like, yesterday.

Unless you're a weirdo like me who realised very early that I wanted freedom more than anything else, you may struggle with this too. We could call this *The Millennial Mindset.*

It could be due to our lack of life experience, or that our identities are not as well solidified yet. Maybe it's being constantly exposed to what other people have and do on social media. We're relentlessly comparing our lives to everyone elses' to see how we stack up.

For that reason, it's worth questioning how much time we spend consuming news and scrolling on social media. Our mental health (and happiness) is best served by turning down the noise and taking a break from technology. This gives our minds a chance to cleanse themselves from these often toxic influences.

"Comparison is the thief of joy." – *Theodore Roosevelt*

For some reason, the average Millennial's default setting seems to be, "I want to do everything/go everywhere/meet everyone/buy everything/experience all there is." And that means we have a really hard time choosing between things.

On the other hand, older folks have realised something powerful: **everything cannot be equally important.** Our job is to prioritise and choose what matters.

You can't have it all. You have to choose. Many of the goals I listed earlier are in opposition to each other. If we try to achieve both at the same time, we probably won't get the full benefits of either. So, what can we do?

Decide on Your Top Priorities

Sounds simple, right? But almost nobody consciously does it. Most of us just cruise through life, wandering in whichever direction takes our fancy at the time, hoping things turn out for the best.

But it's your life we're talking about. This shit is important!

What truly matters for you? Starting a family? Having a gorgeous wedding? Travelling the world? Having complete control of your time? Starting your own business?

Get crystal clear about where your money, time and focus should go, and why. Remember, everyone's situation is different. Try to not have expectations around what your journey *should* be like. It's your life, nobody else's.

Decide on your own priorities and ignore the influence of others. You'll naturally have multiple things you want to do, experience, and accomplish. But deciding on your top priorities is crucial. This helps you ensure your attention and actions are in line with your highest value goals.

Once you do this, everything becomes easier. Anytime you feel scattered or frustrated, you can revisit your priorities. This helps you refocus, make changes, and get your ship back on course.

"If you chase two rabbits, you catch none." – *Russian proverb*

Where to from Here?

If Financial Independence is your top priority at this point, then things are straightforward. But maybe you decide that getting married and having kids is more important right now. In that case, you can be happy about the lower income and higher spending that typically goes with it.

Saying that, having kids and reaching FI is not incompatible. There are plenty of people in the FI community well on their way to freedom (or already there), who have kids. Weddings don't have to be expensive either. It's totally possible to have a beautiful, small, and memorable wedding.

It may even be better for your marriage! In a 2014 Social Science Research Network study, they found a clear correlation between money spent on the event and marriage duration. More expensive weddings were associated with a higher divorce rate. Don't get me wrong, if you want a big wedding, that's fine. But make that a conscious decision, rather than an obligation. The same goes for travel. If it's one of your highest priorities, then have a travel budget built into your yearly spending.

Even though I said you can't have it all, I'm also contradicting myself. Because while you may be choosing other priorities over FI right now, you can still do those things while building the future life you want. It just means your progress will be slower. But if you're clear on what you're doing and are happier along the way, you won't even care.

What Does This Look Like in Practice?

Suppose a couple is torn between going all-in on pursuing FI or getting married/having kids. Let's say the second option wins, but they still really want to reach FI. Here's two options...

Option 1: get married and have kids, while keeping the costs under control. Accept a lower savings rate due to higher spending and lower income for a while. At this point, they'll be happily enjoying their little family unit. And if they keep their life simple, they'll still be able to save and make the most of time with bub. After a few years, bub will be nearing school-age, so they can start getting serious about FI again by ramping up work and savings.

Option 2: shoot for (say) 5 years of hardcore saving up front to smash the mortgage or build investments. Then switch to part-time work while raising kids. At this point, the couple is in a good financial position so they can cruise while enjoying the early years with their children. A bit later, work and savings can be increased as desired, eventually taking this family all the way to FI.

Right now, the important part is deciding your priorities and developing a plan of action. Once you work this out, any stress and FOMO should melt away. Oh, and forget what everyone else is doing (they're just following each other and winging it anyway!). Focus on what YOU want.

Some Thoughts on Regret

In some ways, regret is inevitable. We all look back at what we could have done, rather than what we did. But if we're making conscious choices about our lives and where we're going, there's little reason for regret.

Why? Because we made the best choice for us, based on the information and motivations we had at the time.

Contrast that with someone who is just drifting through life, following their peer group and the standard script of what they're 'supposed' to do. Those people end up with the most regret. They didn't have the courage to think for themselves and decide what future to create.

When we're unclear on our direction, FOMO rears its ugly head. But getting clear on our key priorities forces us to figure out what matters. And that makes sticking to our plans so much easier.

I strongly believe achieving a certain level of financial freedom should be our first focus. Because, as we discussed in chapter three, reducing the need to work gives us more time and energy for the other important aspects of our lives.

Final Thoughts

You might've noticed a lot of discussion around philosophy and mindset for what is supposed to be a personal finance book. That's for good reason. It's not the 'how to' that people struggle with. It's the stuff going on in our heads. That's why our mindset is the most important thing we can develop.

It may sound odd, but nothing much changes in the realm of human experience. Ancient philosophy is just as useful today as it was thousands of years ago. In fact, I'd argue it's more important than ever, considering that so many people are struggling with identity, direction, outside pressure, internal conflict, and figuring out what to care about.

But now that we've mastered our mindset and we're completely dominating our personal finances, it's time to talk about investing. After all, we need a place to put all this cash we're saving!

8

Property vs Shares for Financial Independence

"If you don't find a way to make money in your sleep, you will work until you die." – *Warren Buffett*

You're probably thinking, "we're finally at the exciting part!" And it's true, in this chapter we'll discuss which investments are best suited to fund our financial independence.

Before you invest though, make sure you have cleared all your personal debts. Credit cards, personal loans, and so on. All gone? Excellent. Your mortgage is fine to keep for now. We'll discuss this in more detail later. For those of you with education debt (HECS/HELP), that's okay to leave too, given it is indexed to inflation (equal to a low interest rate).

At this point, I trust you've also got a healthy cash cushion or emergency fund. This helps you leave your investments untouched should you happen to need a source of money in the case of a job loss or other unexpected event. You can now invest with a *I'm owning this forever* mentality. So, let's get stuck into it.

The first question you probably have is, "what should I invest in?"

For all the weird things you might see on the internet these days, the two main asset classes to build long term wealth are still shares and property. These are the most reliable and fundamentally sound investments. They're also a core pillar of society: businesses and buildings. Can you imagine a world without either?

There's endless debate over which is the 'best' asset class. Both have their own strengths and weaknesses, so it depends on what you're trying to achieve. I've invested in both shares and property over many years, so I feel like I can offer a more balanced view than many people.

With that said, I'm going to save you some time. For our purposes, I believe shares are better for most people trying to create freedom through passive income.

This is from someone who thought property was the best thing since sliced bread in my early investing days. But I learned some important lessons on my journey. What I'm about to share is what I wish someone had told me when I started.

My Light Bulb Moment

As we grew our property portfolio, we eventually hit a wall. The lending environment changed, and we could no longer increase our borrowing. At the same time, I began to think more about how we would live off the portfolio.

By this point, we had built a healthy net worth through high savings and decent investment returns. The problem? It was tied up in assets delivering no passive income after mortgages and other costs were accounted for.

Even if we ended up with multiple paid-off properties, the surprising amount of expenses involved meant that living off rental income wasn't going to work. Yes, it's doable, but it's far less lucrative than it sounds (more on that later).

That's when I decided to look at other options for creating an income stream to live on. As it turns out, there was one asset class right under my nose the whole time. I'd just chosen to ignore it, because it was confusing and, if I'm honest, a little scary.

I'm talking about Australian shares. The reason I didn't feel comfortable investing in shares (like many people) was because, frankly, I didn't understand it. But after opening my mind and doing lots of reading, a light bulb went off in my head:

We needed much less wealth to retire than I previously thought if our savings were just parked in the right place.

Aussie shares pay attractive dividends and come with generous tax credits which boost income further. Shifting to shares is why we're free from mandatory work today, with a growing portfolio of income-producing assets, rather than being stuck at work for another 10 years, stubbornly trying to create the same level of freedom from property.

To most people, shares are scary, risky, and so on. I get it, trust me. So, to ease those concerns, let's peel back the curtain and discuss the key benefits of shares and how they differ from property.

Key Benefits of Shares

Easy to get started

Shares have low up-front costs. You can get started with just $500 (or even less). It costs less than $10 in brokerage fees to buy or sell. Investing in property, however, requires tens of thousands as a deposit (say $50k to buy a $500k property), plus tens of thousands in stamp duty and other settlement costs. To sell, you'll be up for tens of thousands more in agent's fees and other charges.

No need to take on debt

You can build your share portfolio entirely with cash savings, adding to your investments every month. This means your portfolio will provide a positive income stream from day one, which will get bigger every year as you add savings and reinvest your dividends. With property, you'll typically need to take on large amounts of debt to get started.

Simple and effective

Investing in an index fund gives you ownership of hundreds (or thousands) of companies, with little homework required. Property requires you to research different areas, property types, price points, rental returns, demographic and population trends to make sure the property you're buying is a good choice.

Time efficient

Once you buy shares, there's nothing to do except keep buying and watch your dividends roll in. All the companies you're invested in take care of themselves, so the admin is very passive. With property, you'll need to be on top of cashflow and debt repayments. You'll also need to liaise with the property manager to deal with repairs, vacancies, improvements, and more.

Extremely diversified

You can easily and cheaply invest in a huge collection of different businesses in one single share fund. This spreads your risk around, with exposure to different companies, sectors, and even countries. With property, the huge amount of capital tied up in each asset means it's a highly concentrated bet with little room for error.

Low ongoing costs

For a diversified share fund, the management fees are very low: typically below 0.3% per annum, and often much cheaper. Property has an enormous level of ongoing costs: council rates, water rates, strata fees (for units), building insurance, landlord insurance, management fees, leasing fees, vacancies, repairs, land tax, improvements. While few people like to admit it, these typically gobble up 35-50% of the rental income. The initial *and* ongoing costs of owning investment properties are massively under-estimated.

Income with tax credits

Dividends from Aussie companies come with franking credits: a credit you get for tax the company has already paid. This reduces the tax owing on your dividends and results in tax refunds for people in a low tax bracket (like retirees). Note: this is quite different from tax *deductions*, which I'll explain in a minute.

Maximum flexibility

You can sell off a chunk of shares and have that money in your account within two days. It's hard to do that with property! This is extremely handy at any time, but especially when you're living off your portfolio.

Healthy long term returns

Shares let you benefit from the best businesses in the world, along with new technology, innovation, and human endeavour. In most countries, shares have the highest long-term returns of any asset class. (Although property in most parts of Australia has also performed incredibly well).

Total Return On Equities Since 1900

Domestic currency, annualised

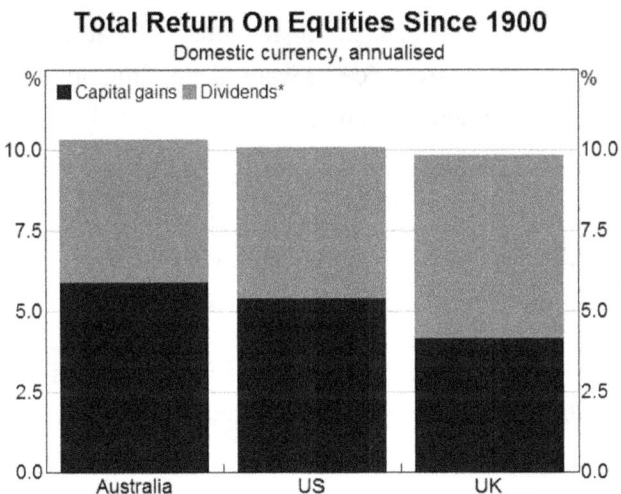

Source: RBA

Let's discuss the common arguments against investing in shares, along with my responses. We'll also hold up the benefits of property to a healthy level of scrutiny, which is almost never done inside the real-estate-religion of Australia.

"The share market is just a big casino."

Where does this 'casino' label come from? A few things. Firstly, the news reports each day whether the market went up or down, and we have no idea why. Secondly, there's the panicky stories about an 'impending crash', or 'market sell-off', or 'billions wiped out'. These are often accompanied by visions of frantic Wall Street traders yelling and pulling their hair out.

No wonder we think it's a casino! But let's think about it. What is the share market? It's simply a place where we can buy and sell slices of businesses.

In the old days, people used to physically exchange papers of ownership. These days, it's an online marketplace, which is more efficient, effortless, and unbelievably cheap to transact. The fact that we're able to buy and sell at any time of the day, at any price we want, depending on how we feel, is what causes shares to fluctuate in price.

"Property is stable, shares are so volatile."

Consider this: if property was transacted the same way shares are, you'd see much more volatility than you do now. Imagine trying to sell your house every weekend. The turnout, mood, and offers would vary quite a lot. Some weeks people will fight over your property. Other weeks, there'll be little interest, or low-ball offers only.

There's an important fact which is overlooked about property price indices. The 'price growth' we hear about includes all renovations, extensions, improvements, and new builds. People spend considerable amounts on their homes, re-doing kitchens and bathrooms, putting in nice gardens, new floors, pools, gazebos, the list is endless.

A $700,000 home – which sells for $770,000 two years later – could have undergone $70,000 worth of renovations. But the 10% growth in sales price is all that gets recorded. This creates a misleading upward bias to the data.

Because most people approach property with a long-term view, nobody worries about short-term price drops. If someone offers you 10% less for your house than you paid a few months ago, you can freak out and think that you've lost money, or you can simply say "no thanks – I'm in it for the long term."

The same thinking also applies to shares. Just because you see a certain price doesn't mean you need to care about it. At first, it can be tough to accept this. But remember: all that price tells you is what buyers and sellers were agreeing on for that day.

"But what if it crashes?"

The share market has delivered attractive returns for a long time. But to earn these returns, you must be able to stomach big drops from time to time. Possibly 30-50%.

These are uncommon events, and nobody knows when they'll occur. History suggests maybe once every 10-20 years. But the world keeps turning, humans keep innovating, and the market keeps rising over time.

Since 1900, the total return from Australian equities would have multiplied an investor's money by more than 1,000 times *after* inflation. This is compound interest in action. $1,000 becomes over $1,000,000.

Cumulative Real Returns*
Log scale, 1 January 1900 = 100

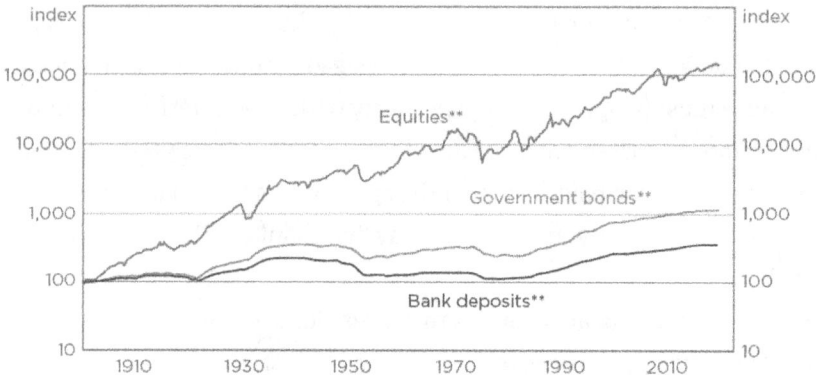

Source: RBA

Remember, a downturn creates *opportunity*. When shares fall heavily, you have the chance to buy more shares at lower prices.

If you're building a portfolio, that's exactly what you want! And if you're living mostly off the income from your portfolio, with a little flexibility, you can basically ignore it.

Isn't it funny how the media loves to report the end of the world, yet they never mention the enormous upwards march of progress?

"You can't improve shares, but you can improve property through renovations."

Adding value through renovations is unique to property. And if you do the work yourself, it can work out well indeed. But this trick has diminishing returns, and there's risk involved. If the market falls while you're renovating, you'll be lucky to break even.

And some renovations aren't even optional. As property owners, we're forced to repair, maintain, and even upgrade the property over time, just to maintain market rents. If we don't, nobody will want to live there!

With shares, management teams are working every day to make the company more valuable, by finding new ways to expand, innovate, create products, build greater loyalty, lower costs, and outsmart the competition.

This means new revenue streams, additional customers, and stronger brand power. That's how businesses grow and create value. Sounds like an improvement to me, with no work required on our part.

"But shares aren't even real things. I can see and touch my investment property."

This one is very natural, if maybe a bit silly. If you live in the big cities of Australia, look at the CBD. See the names on those skyscrapers. All very real businesses, wouldn't you say?

Think of your local Woolies or Coles. Ever driven on a toll-road? Visited a Westfield, Bunnings, or your local bank? They all seem pretty real to me.

There's hundreds of businesses you would use or walk past every week without realising that they're owned by a company listed on the ASX. Now think about your smartphone, computer, and the apps you use. Apple, Amazon, Google, Facebook, and the endless list of large global companies that have built tangible products and platforms which we've grown to rely on.

Where did these things come from, if not real businesses? Try strolling up to caress the exterior of your investment property. Your tenants will likely call the police! Do it at your local Coles and people just think you're a weirdo (I've only done it once – shut up).

"But my mate lost heaps of money with shares."

You know the term I hate the most? Dabbling. When you hear someone is 'dabbling' in shares, you can guarantee they have absolutely no idea what they're doing. And 99 times out of 100, that ends badly. For some reason, when people get into shares, common sense goes out the window. It turns from investing into gambling. Looking for the next big winner. Taking a hot tip from someone at the pub. Does anyone really believe that's a realistic way to build wealth?

We love to gamble in Australia. Unfortunately, many newbies approach shares like a glorified version of the lotto. Buy a few shares and hope one of them goes to the moon. But *that's not investing.* So I'm not surprised your mate/relative/work colleague lost money!

The share market is excellent at taking people who don't know what they're doing, then separating them from their money. But that's down to our individual behaviour, not the market itself.

The main way people lose money in shares is by trading, not diversifying properly, or having a timeframe measured in months, rather than decades. According to data provider Market Index, since 1900 the ASX has delivered positive returns in 81% of all years. The longer your timeframe, the higher that percentage goes, hitting 100% positive returns over any historical ten-year timeframe.

If the share market really was a casino, those are incredible odds!

"But individual companies can go broke."

Absolutely true! There can be more longevity in well-located real estate compared to shares. The truth is, individual shares are quite risky. Companies often go broke and fall out of existence. That won't happen with an individual property in a half-decent location.

How do we fix this? Diversification. The more companies you own, the less reliant you are on any one company remaining prosperous. More on this later.

"But I have no control."

Often this is an emotional factor. If you buy shares, you don't control the actions of the people running it, or the results of the business. But having direct control doesn't mean you'll get a better outcome.

I'm 100% in control of my Perth properties. That wasn't the slightest bit helpful when the market effectively went nowhere for 10 years. On the flipside, I'm 100% *responsible* for them. Meaning: the burden of cost, issues, and administration comes back to me.

With shares, CEOs and management teams run the companies we invest in. So yes, we give up control to them. The upside is, it's far more passive from our end. And with a big basket of companies, one crazy CEO doing the wrong thing won't damage our portfolio.

"But property has great tax benefits like negative gearing and depreciation."

It's often pointed out that while Aussie shares have franking credits, property has depreciation benefits. But these two things aren't equal. The reason you're allowed to deduct the value of your property depreciating is because its condition is literally worsening with every year. While it makes for a nice tax deduction, it also means – yep, you guessed it – future expenses.

Another key difference: depreciation is a tax *deduction*, whereas franking is a tax *credit*. One is a genuine cost you can use to reduce your tax. The other is real cash with your name on it, sitting at the tax office.

Finally, you can also negatively gear with shares, so that's not an exclusive benefit to property.

The Income Potential

Shares require no extra cash to keep producing income. The money you receive is yours to keep. In this way, rents and dividends couldn't be more different.

Rental properties come with many costs: council rates, water rates, management fees, leasing fees, inspection fees, land tax, strata fees, building insurance, landlord insurance, repairs and maintenance, upgrades over time, and vacancies.

Any honest property investor knows how much this adds up. But it's often tolerated because the focus is capital growth (we'll discuss this in a minute).

After several years of property investing, I thought I knew the numbers. But one day I decided to audit my properties. I was shocked to find that when all expenses were added up and averaged out, these suckers were costing a lot more than I thought, with close to half the rental income being hoovered up in expenses.

Consider a 4% rental yield. The above costs would comfortably erode 40% of your rent. That leaves you with a net yield of maybe 2.4%.

Compare this to a 4% dividend yield, which has no expenses attached. In fact, dividends from Aussie shares come with franking credits (a credit for tax the company has paid on this money before paying you a dividend). These tax credits often add 1% or more to the dividend return.

So, your 4% dividend could become 5% (or more) when franking credits are included. This covers some of the tax owing on your dividend income, or if you're in a low tax situation, it becomes a tax refund.

At first, the two yields look the same. But Aussie dividend income ends up being *double* the rental income. To get 5% rental income after costs, you'd need a yield of around 9%.

Can you get that? Maybe. But it would probably have to be an extremely cheap (higher risk) location, likely with terrible growth prospects, and perhaps questionable tenants. What about commercial property? Well, these have higher yields. But then your wealth is concentrated in one or two assets, and it's common for commercial properties to be vacant for months or a year between tenants.

Basically, shares tend to be more efficient at producing income than property, once everything is accounted for. You could argue that rents are more stable than dividends. That's often true. But rents can and do fall too. Even well-located areas in capital cities can experience rental and price declines.

What about Growing Passive Income?

Even considering the yield differences, are rents and dividends likely to have the same growth?

Personally, I believe dividends will grow quicker than rents over time. Why? Well, for one, companies reinvest some of their earnings to help grow future profits and dividends.

Next, rents (and property prices) can't grow faster than wages forever. If they do, people can't afford accommodation. On that same point, wages can't grow faster than company profits forever, or companies would go bankrupt. So, in a simplified way, company profits tend to sit at the top of the food chain. This is where value is created. Efficiency and innovation enables companies to pay higher wages, which allows people to pay more for property. While both rents and dividends should outpace inflation, company profits (and therefore dividends) seem likely to grow a little more.

Now, I know when people mention 'growth' in regards to property, they're really talking about using leverage to magnify their returns. Let's open that can of worms now.

"But you can leverage property to make massive returns!"

This is undeniably true. And it's a large reason why many people invest in property over shares. Put your deposit down to buy a property which grows in value, and you make a huge return on the amount you invested. Leverage can be a powerful multiplier. What I will say is this: the returns are not what they first seem, and they do come with a catch.

I'll use an example to show you what I mean. Let's say you buy a $500,000 property with a 15% deposit ($75,000). For simplicity, I'll assume steady growth, and an interest-only loan which you don't have to pay down. I've also (generously) assumed the property pays for itself with no out-of-pocket expenses, while ignoring stamp duty and other up-front costs.

In the beginning, your return on equity is huge. Because of debt, your return is magnified. But as time goes on, it becomes less impressive. Take a look:

Property value	Loan amount	Your equity	Capital growth 3%	Return on equity
$500,000	$425,000	$75,000	$15,000	20%
$600,000	$425,000	$175,000	$18,000	10.3%
$750,000	$425,000	$325,000	$22,500	6.9%
$900,000	$425,000	$475,000	$27,000	5.8%

Can you see what's happening? Over time, as your equity in the property grows, your leverage decreases. And as leverage decreases, so does your rate of return. Those magnified returns we all get so excited about actually go down.

Of course, the property will eventually become positive cashflow which adds to returns. And yes, capital growth may well be higher than this. But it could also be lower. And the property could easily produce negative cashflow, depending on interest rates, yields, and expenses. I could keep making it more complicated, but I trust that the basic principle is clear.

Looking at returns this way is incredibly important, yet rarely done. Whatever equity we have invested in a property is money that could be invested elsewhere. We always need to compare this to other options to see if there's an 'opportunity cost'.

This also tells us something else: the only way to sustain high returns from property is to stay highly leveraged. And that means working forever. Why? Because highly leveraged property in Australia generally produces no (or negative) income after mortgage repayments and costs. Eventually that situation has to change.

To retire, this will mean selling assets, paying capital gains tax, agents fees, closing costs, and then investing into other assets which are more effective at producing income.

This can be a hard pill to swallow, since it cuts into the gains you've built up while also reducing the size of your asset base. It feels like a step backwards to sell to invest elsewhere, so few do it.

Leverage and Growth

You might think I'm being unfair, because there are other ways to approach property investment. But I've framed the discussion this way because most property investing in Australia is simply a bet on capital city price growth, using leverage.

This has made countless people fantastically wealthy. That said, it's not an easy ticket to riches. There can be long periods where property prices are flat or fall. I've been on the receiving end of this in Perth, where prices stalled for over a decade.

Other cities are not immune to this either, including the poster child of housing performance, Sydney. Periods of 5 or more years with no growth do happen, especially if you pay too much.

And remember, up-front costs are substantial. Tens of thousands for stamp duty and other costs, and sometimes tens of thousands more for

Lender's Mortgage Insurance (which you usually need to pay if you have less than a 20% deposit).

In most cases, you need a few years of growth *just to break even.* Add in unexpected issues like costly repairs, extended vacancy, or a poor performing market, and you can easily be looking at 5-7 years before you make a single dollar of positive return.

And if you do get decent price growth, you'll later need to cash out and take your equity to invest in an asset which produces better income. My point is, if your timeframe is 10 years or less, it might not be enough time to earn a good return if you get unlucky with growth.

Don't get me wrong, the share market has horrible periods, too. And yes, the ability to leverage isn't the same. The upside is that shares provide increasing passive income every year as you build your portfolio, which is more enjoyable and less stressful. It's also a more reliable way to start creating freedom, one chunk at a time.

The Past is Not the Future

> "But property grows at 7% per year, so your example of 3% capital growth is ridiculous!"

Are you sure? It's important to realise *how* prices grow, rather than make assumptions about *how much* they grow. There are numerous reasons this growth rate occurred historically, which is unlikely to keep repeating.

- **Wage growth and inflation used to be much higher.** Of course property can grow at 7% per year when incomes are growing at 7%. But what about when wages grow at 3%?
- **Increase in household debt.** As interest rates came down from 15% to 2%, we borrowed more and pushed up prices. This fuelled a lot of the growth in house prices over the last 40 years. How much lower can mortgage rates go?

- **More women working full-time.** This was a large boost to household incomes, increasing our borrowing power and what we could afford to spend on housing.

The natural limit on property prices is how fast our incomes grow and how much more debt we can take on. At this point I might sound like I'm anti-property investing. I'm not. Frankly, I think well located real estate in Australia will be worth a lot more in the future, so it will remain a sensible and profitable investment option. But expecting prices to grow at historic rates is unrealistic. Is that also true of shares? Possibly, which is why we've used more conservative figures throughout this book:

- I've quoted numbers like 7% annual returns (income, plus growth), rather than the long-term average of 10%.
- Using (lower) world average returns instead of just Australia which has been a standout performer.
- Considering after-inflation returns.
- Building a margin of safety into our plans (more on this in chapter twelve).
- Ignoring the extra income from franking credits, which aren't included in any of the return charts you've seen.

It's true that many new investors tend to overestimate future returns while underestimating possible costs and problems. I've found property investors (myself included) are far more susceptible to this problem. So if you're going down the property path, be conservative with your expectations.

All things considered, for those who want to create freedom and passive income as soon as possible, property may not be the best fit. Aussie real estate is mostly about using debt to build lots of equity. And when that strategy works, you become equity rich, cashflow poor.

Equity Rich, Cashflow Poor

Let's say you become very wealthy using leverage to buy real estate for capital growth. Then what? Building your equity is fantastic on paper. It's tax efficient. The assets do the hard work. You just sit back and watch your wealth compound. But a high net worth may not result in the freedom you'd expect.

Wealth is necessary for financial independence. But being wealthy doesn't mean *you are* financially independent.

Consider a couple with a $2 million paid-off home. You could consider them wealthy. This is a multi-millionaire couple!

While that *sounds* good, it doesn't directly help them achieve FI. Sure, they can probably work part-time now and cruise along. But their 'multi-millionaire' status is not actually what helped them. The fact that they'd paid off their house did.

Why? Because this dramatically reduces their expenses, and therefore, their need to work. Unfortunately, this couple does still have to work to cover their other expenses, since they have no other sources of income.

This scenario of being equity rich, cashflow poor (albeit with smaller numbers) is extremely common in Australia. Especially with traditional age retirees. Our obsession with property almost ensures this is the case.

All Wealth Is Not Equal

Now let's compare two people. One we'll call High Roller Harry. The other we will call Moderately Wealthy Martin. High Roller Harry has a net worth of $3 million. Moderately Wealthy Martin has $1.5 million.

Who is more financially independent? Would you say Harry? I'd say it depends. Since all we know about them is their net worth, we need more information.

What if they both have the same expenses of $50,000 per year? Then, clearly Harry is better off, right? I'd say we *still* can't draw a conclusion. After all, Harry could have all his money tied up in a fancy $2 million home, an impressive boat, and a couple of luxury cars.

In this case, he has very little freedom and still needs to work to cover his living expenses. Harry is fully reliant on his job because he has no other income streams.

What about Martin? Well, his entire net worth happens to be invested in shares. He rents his home, so there's no money tied up in home ownership.

With a portfolio of diversified shares, he can produce an income stream of around $60,000 per year (4%). Because Martin's net worth is working hard for him in investments, his living expenses are fully covered. Therefore, he is financially independent. Despite having half the amount of wealth, I'd argue Martin is in a stronger financial position.

Since Martin is renting and doesn't have any status symbols, people probably think he's less financially successful than Harry. But the truth is that Martin has complete control over his life. He's free to spend his time doing whatever he likes. Contrast this to Harry, who has no freedom at all, despite being far wealthier on paper.

So it's not all about net worth and equity. It's about what type of lifestyle that equity is producing for you. A million dollars can mean complete financial independence, or it can mean not much at all.

The point is, don't tie up all your money in assets that aren't helping you gain more freedom. Make sure you park it in the right place!

Now, you might say that wasn't a fair comparison because High Roller Harry wasn't an investor like Martin. OK, let's assume Harry is an investor too.

Equity-Rich Investor

We'll ignore the toys for the sake of this example and look strictly at assets. Since he loves owning property, we'll give Harry a good-sized property portfolio worth $3 million, with $2 million of debt. This means he has $1m of equity in his portfolio, and of course, his $2 million paid-off home.

All up, Harry has $5 million of property and $2 million of debt. His net equity in property assets is $3 million. That's pretty damn good. You'd be hard pressed to find an Aussie who wouldn't be envious.

But how financially independent is he? Let's see.

His property portfolio is in well-located capital-city areas and has a rental yield of around 3.5%. After expenses, the net yield for Harry's portfolio is around 2%.

This equates to $60,000 per year on his $3m of investment properties. Assuming a mortgage rate of 3%, the interest on his $2m of debt amounts to $60,000 per year.

So ultimately, despite owning a total of $5 million of real estate, including multiple investments and multi-millionaire status, his total passive income is... zero dollars. With no investment income, Harry is still entirely reliant on his work income to cover his personal expenses. And if interest rates rise, he's footing the bill for that too. We've also been generous and assumed he's not having to pay principal-and-interest on his mortgages, which would mean higher repayments.

Don't get me wrong, Harry is very rich on paper. But he still has little control over how he spends his time. All this equity is providing him no passive income and no freedom.

Of course, he could sell some of his portfolio and start using his equity to create income. But almost nobody does this since it means paying Capital Gains Tax and having a smaller portfolio of assets.

Since property tends to be viewed as a sacred asset that should never be sold, countless Aussies are too scared to use their equity to achieve real freedom. Which is a shame, because while High-Roller Harry has plenty of options, Moderately Wealthy Martin is in a better position.

Because Martin focused on building passive income using his savings, instead of leveraging up to build equity, he's now financially independent, despite having a vastly lower net worth.

Somehow, I don't think Martin cares that Harry is richer. As Monday morning rolls around, Martin has the greatest luxury of all – time – while Harry contemplates another week at the office.

Harry is richer on paper. Martin is richer in life.

Focus on building passive income rather than the 'paper wealth' of equity.

Shares Are Better for FI

If we want to start creating freedom quickly, we do that by using all our available cash to create an accessible income stream from shares. My partner and I are retired today because we decided to bite the bullet and begin selling down our property portfolio to put that equity into shares.

For some, this may look like bailing out, or not being fully committed to our initial plan. After all, some treat a property portfolio as a big shiny badge of honour. But our plan was not to accumulate properties forever and build mammoth pools of equity. The goal wasn't wealth for the sake of wealth. Since the very beginning, our plan was to get our lives back as soon as possible.

It just so happens that along our journey we found a better way to reach our ultimate goal. And if that meant accepting that we needed to change our strategy, then that was fine with me.

Today, we're better off for being open-minded and changing strategies. As you can see, it's not about how much equity you have, or even being a multi-millionaire. It's all about what your equity is providing for you.

Final Thoughts

Let me be clear: property can be an excellent long-term investment. If you still want to take the real estate road, that's totally okay. Or if you want to invest in shares *and* property, that's cool, too.

It's my opinion that investing in shares is more effective at helping you control your time sooner. Because the truth is, with a good savings rate, you don't need leverage to create financial independence.

Too many people become wedded to property out of fear or ego. As a result, they miss out on retiring earlier, or creating a better income stream from their wealth, simply because they're reluctant to make the switch.

Interesting side note: I've heard from numerous people who have switched from property to shares after building knowledge and experience in both assets. But I know none who have switched from shares to property.

OK, let's bring it full circle. Here's a summary of the benefits of shares and how this lines up with the positive attributes we want from our investments:

- Simple to understand.
- Highly diversified.
- Easy to get started.
- Truly passive and hands off.
- Very little possible complications.
- Low transaction costs.
- Low ongoing costs.
- Liquid and flexible (access money quickly).
- Positive income producing.
- Solid long-term returns.
- Tax effective.
- No debt needed.

At this point, my views may look too tilted to one side. But none of this is written out of ignorance. Remember, I'm one of the few people who has invested in both asset classes for many years. I also don't have a job reliant on either one. I'm just a guy who retired early and is writing about the things he's learned along the way.

So, if shares look like the better option, which shares are we supposed to buy? In the next chapter, we'll discuss how to build a share portfolio for passive income and long-term growth. It's a lot easier than you might think. I'll also share how I invest and the pros and cons of different approaches.

9

Simplified Share Investing

"Simplicity is the master key to financial success." - *John Bogle*

As I pointed to in the previous chapter, an effective method for investing in shares is to buy a big basket of them. And the biggest basket of shares you can buy is an index fund which tracks the market of a given country.

For example, the ASX 300 is a basket of the biggest 300 listed companies in Australia. The ASX 300 provides broad exposure to Aussie shares as it represents 82% of the total equity market at the time of writing.

By investing in an index fund which holds these 300 companies, you benefit from the growth and income of these businesses over time.

Broad index funds like this are weighted according to each company's market value. More is invested in big companies compared to smaller companies.

For example, at the time of writing, Commonwealth Bank (CBA) represents about 7% of the Aussie market's value. So about 7% of an ASX 300 index fund is invested in CBA. Telstra, on the other hand, makes up 2% of the market's value, and therefore, the index.

Here's a few reasons why index funds are an excellent choice for long term share investing.

Low Cost

Index funds come with the lowest management fees of any funds out there. Why does this matter? Well, one of the best predictors of a share fund's performance is its fees.

High fee funds may have great sounding strategies, but after fees, investors are usually worse off. Not only that, but fees add up over time (I'll share some crazy numbers to put this in perspective in chapter ten).

Make no mistake, costs are a big drag on your returns as an investor.

As John Bogle (the founder of Vanguard and creator of the world's first index fund) was fond of saying, "in the investment world, you get what you don't pay for."

Low Turnover

Another hidden drag on returns is tax. Investing in funds which have high turnover (meaning they frequently buy and sell) will incur more taxes than the simple buy and hold strategy that index funds employ.

More taxes mean less money compounding for you. Companies move up and down the ranks within the top 300, as some prosper and grow larger, while others shrink. But all this happens naturally inside the fund with no unnecessary transactions needing to take place.

Diversification

Index funds that track the entire market are quite diversified because they own every major company, with a range of sectors and industries.

This is handy because different sectors do well at various times. When healthcare is strong, financial companies may be struggling, or mining is booming while consumer companies are lagging.

Owning lots of different businesses is better than relying on a few. With an index fund, you don't have to figure out which companies or sectors are going to do well. You own everything. If healthcare or technology companies become increasingly large over time, that will be reflected in the index.

Automatically Updated

Related to the above, index funds are updated each quarter to reflect the index it is tracking – the ASX 300, for example.

Over time, some companies will fall out of the top 300 and be replaced with other smaller but growing companies. Dying companies are weeded out as they shrink and become irrelevant.

At all times, an ASX 300 index fund will reflect the biggest 300 companies in Australia. That's true in 2022, as well as 2072. This provides confidence in the long-term viability of your investment.

Picking Winners is Hard

Perhaps the most underappreciated point. As you might guess, not all companies have the same returns. But the difference in outcomes is mind-blowing. Put simply, the majority of stocks underperform the market average.

Not only that, but a small percentage of companies become massive long-term winners which just about carry the entire market. Miss a few and it's almost certain you'll do worse than owning an index fund.

One study by Longboard Asset Management from 1989 to 2015 showed that 20% of US stocks were responsible for the market's 1,200% gain over that time. Incredibly, the other 80% of stocks had a collective return of 0%, with four out of ten stocks experiencing a *negative return.*

The odds of repeatedly finding and holding long-term winners is slim. But because of the previous point, a broad index is guaranteed to benefit from the big winners. Most active investors underperform because of this reason: it's a hard game.

Competition is Fierce

There are thousands of analysts and professional investors pouring over every detail of these companies that we're casually glancing at. This makes markets reasonably efficient. When new information (good or bad) comes out it's quickly incorporated into the share price.

Think of share prices as a running estimate of what everybody thinks a company is worth. Prices always move because opinions and information changes. The people who pick stocks for a living are smart, hardworking people, all trying to earn high returns.

It's unlikely we can turn over a few rocks, skim through presentations and have a better idea of a company's value and future prospects.

Harvesting Business Returns

The great part is, we don't need to do anything fancy with our investing. When we buy shares in a company or an index fund, we're essentially piggy backing on the success of those businesses. Our long-term returns are basically driven by two things: dividends the company pays (from its profits), and the growth in earnings over time (which makes the company more valuable and allows them to pay larger dividends in the future).

The following table shows the maths behind how this works in practice:

Year	Business assets	Profit (R.O.E)	Dividend	Retained earnings
1	100.00	10.0	5.00	5.00
2	105.00	10.5	5.25	5.25
3	110.25	11.0	5.50	5.50
4	115.75	11.6	5.80	5.80
5	121.55	12.2	6.10	6.10
6	127.65	12.8	6.40	6.40
7	134.05			

Source: IML and Peter Thornhill

Each year the company makes profit and pays a dividend. It retains and reinvests the rest of its earnings into the business which leads to future growth. This is why the stock market goes up over time and what drives the long-term returns in our chart from earlier.

When we buy an ASX index fund, for example, we're hitching our wagon to the future success of Australian companies as a whole. But it's not just Australia. We can buy index funds which hold companies around the world.

Now that we've covered why index funds are a sensible choice for long term investing, let's look at some of the different options for building a portfolio.

Investing in Index Funds

Rather than overwhelm you with pages of details, I'll simply share two examples of index funds I own personally.

Among many others, these are popular options among Aussies wanting to invest for the long term in a diversified portfolio of Australian and global shares.

- Australian shares: VAS. Largest 300 Aussie companies. Managed by Vanguard.
- International shares: VGS. Largest 1500 Global companies. Managed by Vanguard.

The global shares index fund includes countries such as the US and other developed markets like the UK, Japan, Canada, and Europe.

Because the US is the biggest global market, it makes up around 70% of VGS (at the time of writing). Not included are 'emerging' markets like China, Taiwan, India, and more.

The above options are very low-cost ETFs (exchange-traded funds), which can be bought with any online brokerage account. Management fees are low at 0.1% - 0.2% per annum, and are automatically deducted from the fund's returns. Interestingly, management fees on broad index funds like these also have a history of becoming cheaper over time.

The two funds mentioned are just one example of an effective and efficient way to invest in Australian and international shares for the long term. For transparency, a large chunk of my portfolio these days is made up of these two Vanguard funds. I do have other investments, but I like the simplicity and diversification of this simple combo.

But it can be even simpler than this.

Investing in 'All-In-One' Diversified Index Funds

It's now possible to invest in a single ETF which has multiple index funds inside it. These one-fund portfolio solutions contain all the biggest and best Aussie and global companies wrapped up in a single parcel. Here are two examples:

VDHG (Vanguard Diversified High Growth)

This fund invests in a mixture of Aussie shares (approx. 35-40%) and global shares (approx. 50-55%), as well as some fixed interest bonds (10%).

DHHF (Betashares Diversified All Growth)

This fund invests in a mix of Aussie shares (approx. 35-40%) and the remainder in global shares (60-65%). DHHF is 100% invested in shares, with no fixed interest investments like bonds.

Fees for these all-in-one funds are a little higher, but still total around 0.3% per annum or less. And it's worth mentioning that these two funds invest in an *even larger* basket than our previous examples, because they also include emerging markets and small global companies.

Now, there are pros and cons to building your own portfolio versus using a one-fund option like this.

Why DIY is Better:

- You can choose how much you want invested in each fund. The one-fund portfolios are already set, you can't adjust them to suit yourself.
- Lower fees. The separate index funds come with lower management fees than the all-in-one options. This adds up over time.
- You can optimise what you buy and sell. As you add to your portfolio, you can add more to whichever fund is underperforming while prices are low. With a single fund, you can't do that.

Why the One-Fund Option Is Better:

- Having a one fund portfolio is the ultimate in simplicity.
- Less to manage, less to think about, more peace of mind.
- It may make the investing process and experience more enjoyable.
- With a single fund you probably won't have the urge to tinker or change things around like you might with multiple funds.
- Many people aren't passionate about investing. Even those of us who are don't make the best decisions. The less there is to do, the less chance we have of screwing something up. If you can achieve your financial goals with just one fund, there's a strong argument for going with that.

Paying slightly higher fees for simplicity and peace of mind may sound like an excellent trade-off. Or maybe you think the benefits of choosing your own funds come out on top. Ultimately, there's no right or wrong. Have a think about what's best for you.

To help you think through this decision, let's talk about the benefits of both Aussie and international shares and how we can think about putting a portfolio together.

Asset Allocation

Asset allocation is the breakdown of where you have your money invested. Aussie shares, international shares, property, cash, and so on.

How you choose to invest is a big driver of your long-term returns. For a lower, more stable return, you can keep a good chunk of your savings in cash and invest a modest amount into higher-returning assets like shares. But if you want to earn higher returns, you're typically better off investing as much as you can into shares, and getting used to the ups and downs.

Investing in Australia

People don't usually need convincing of investing in their own country, but here's why you might want to invest in Aussie shares:

- You know and are familiar with many Australian companies: big banks, BHP, Sydney Airport, realestate.com, Wesfarmers (owner of Bunnings & Officeworks).
- Your current and future expenses are in Aussie dollars. Having investments in Australian assets is the easiest way to meet your future needs.
- Aussie shares have higher dividends which are taxed favourably compared to international shares, thanks to franking credits.
- Australia is a wealthy, developed country, with relatively well managed companies, stable institutions, and the rule of law. It's a reasonably safe place to invest.
- Australia has been among the best performing share markets in the world since 1900, along with similar English-speaking, capitalist countries. No guarantee for the future, but this indicates an environment that is good for business and wealth generation.
- Australia has a healthy long term demographic outlook compared to most countries (population growth). Our lifestyle, weather, living standards, social safety nets and environment makes us an attractive destination for skilled migration. That's a long-term tailwind for the economy and the share market.

But nothing is guaranteed. There's always a chance that Australian companies, and maybe the country in general, do poorly over the long term. Which is why it's good to diversify.

Investing Internationally

- Markets outside Australia contain the biggest, most dominant companies in the world: Apple, Amazon, Google, and Microsoft.
- The US makes up over half of the entire world's stock market value. Australia is only a few percent.
- Global markets are rich in industries that we lack, like technology and strong consumer brands such as Nike, Starbucks, and McDonalds. This means more diversification and less reliance on particular industries.
- Overseas (especially the US) is typically where the most exciting innovation happens, and where many of the new potentially world-changing companies are born (like Tesla).
- Global shares tend to have higher growth than Australian shares, since they pay lower dividends and reinvest more of their profits.
- Our money is exposed to other currencies. During market downturns it's common for the Aussie dollar to fall. In this case, our international shares are worth more in comparison. If markets fall together, overseas shares may hold up better, which softens the blow somewhat.

Owning both Aussie and international shares gives you a complementary spread of businesses in many different industries. By not having all your investments in one country, you reduce the risk of poor performance. In this way, global shares can be a great form of insurance.

Combining the Two

I started off with 100% Australian shares because I like the higher dividends that Aussie companies pay.

But I've since come to appreciate the benefits of greater diversification, so I now invest in global shares too. I'm continually impressed by US companies and their sheer dominance in our lives. Frankly, wanting to have a decent chunk of my money invested in those companies is what convinced me the most.

As an interesting side note, a Vanguard study showed that the least volatile portfolio combination of Aussie and international shares was a 50% stake in each. Personally, I like this simple split and it's actually my long-term target.

As I mentioned, global shares (and the earnings they produce) offer exposure to various currencies which move differently from one another. This offers another form of diversification, compared to having solely Australian assets.

If you're investing heavily in global shares, be mindful of currency risk. If all your investments are in other currencies, but your expenses are in Aussie dollars, the currency moving the wrong way could negatively impact your portfolio for many years. Consider having some of your global allocation in funds which are 'hedged' to Australian dollars. One example of this is VGAD (which has the same companies as VGS but is hedged to Australian dollars).

This also adds another layer of complexity and decision-making to your investing, which is not for everyone (myself included). Even discussing this makes me want to invest in a one-fund portfolio and go take a nap!

So, What's the Best Option?

Often, people will claim there is an 'optimal' choice. But they're probably saying that because it's how *they* invest. The truth is, there is no 'best' portfolio. Just get started with whatever makes sense to you.

In all honesty, the best portfolio is the one you can stick with through the ups and downs. Because once you have the basics right, your behaviour as an investor matters more than which funds you invest in.

As Morgan Housel put it: *"If you understand the math behind compounding, you realize the most important question isn't, 'how can I earn the highest returns?' It's, 'what are the best returns I can sustain for the longest period of time?'"*

Take one investor trying to be super smart and chase the highest possible returns. They constantly tweak their portfolio when they see a new idea, or switch strategies when it's not working, and even sell when the market falls.

Now, take a quiet investor who invests consistently into their chosen assets every month. They don't watch the market constantly and they don't care what other people are doing. Our quiet investor simply picked a strategy that lets them sleep well at night. Maybe they don't have the most optimal choices, but I can promise you, the quiet investor will easily outperform the 'smart' investor.

Funnily enough, this is also why some people are truly better off with property. They simply can't get comfortable with the share market. This means they won't be able to hold on long enough to get those compound long term returns.

For those who are unsure or don't want to deal with multiple funds, picking an all-in-one index fund option is likely a good idea. Quite often, a simple option is best.

Having said that, I should at least mention some other simple, cost-effective ways to invest as well. Let's discuss a few now.

Listed Investment Companies (LICs)

LICs invest in an actively managed portfolio of shares.

Some focus on small stocks, value stocks, dividend paying stocks, international stocks, growth stocks, or something else entirely. All LICs have their own management team and aim to deliver healthy returns to shareholders through their chosen strategy.

Many LICs are typically more expensive than ETFs, which we know is a drag on returns. Some will beat the market, but most won't. And while people say 'just pick the good ones', finding the winning investment managers in advance is like trying to pick the winning stocks.

Investing in LICs and other actively managed funds can suit some people.

For whatever reason, some folks simply feel more comfortable knowing there are other humans doing research and hand-picking which companies go into the portfolio. Or maybe they like other strategies better than the robotic 'own everything' approach of index funds.

One advantage of LICs is that they're able to decide what level of dividends to pay to shareholders based on their profit, with the remaining earnings being reinvested just like a normal company. This can help them provide a more reliable income stream to shareholders over time. On the other hand, index funds and other ETFs are structured in a way that forces them to pay out any income they receive.

LICs trade on the stock exchange just like any other share. Each month the LIC reports the value of its portfolio of investments. This value is often different from the share price, which moves around depending on whether people are optimistic or pessimistic about that LIC.

For example, sometimes you'll see an LIC with a portfolio worth $5 per share trading at $4.50 per share. This means the LIC is trading at a 10% discount to the value of its assets. Often this discount is for good reason, like ongoing poor performance. But other times, it's simply the mood of the market. It also happens in the other direction. People might feel optimistic about a strongly performing LIC and bid up its price to $5.50 when its portfolio is only worth $5.

If we like a certain LIC, we can take advantage of this by buying when it's trading at a discount. This can boost your return, since you're getting the same portfolio and income stream for a lower price than usual.

Given LICs hand-pick which companies to buy, they may miss some long-term winners. As a result, there's a fair chance their performance won't match the index. That's the trade-off to keep in mind with actively managed funds.

Because of this, it would be prudent to have these make up a smaller part of a portfolio. Also consider two things: fees (the lower the better), and how long the manager has been following their strategy (the longer the better).

I've invested in a number of these funds over the years and typically targeted these three traits: low fees, long history and a simple strategy.

Some examples of LICs I have owned include Argo Investments (ARG), and Australian Foundation Investment Company (AFI).

I know several people who invest in LICs and are living off their portfolio, who simply prefer the 'hands on' nature of actively managed funds, along with the more stable income stream. We'll talk more about dividends and living off your portfolio later in the book. But now let's talk about another style of investing which has become popular in recent years.

Ethical Funds and ESG Investing

Ethical investing is investing in shares that aim to be of higher moral or ethical standards than other companies. ESG stands for environmental, social, and governance. These are issues companies are measured on to deem them ethical or otherwise.

Ethical investing is commonly marketed as 'do better while doing good'. Investing this way is usually done through active ETFs and index funds. The fund manager applies certain filters to exclude companies: no tobacco, gambling, fossil fuels, mining, alcohol or junk food producers, and so on.

There are all sorts of filters to ensure that your money isn't invested in companies which you disagree with. That sounds pretty good, right? There are definitely a few benefits to this:

- You invest in a way you feel better about and avoid companies you think are harmful.
- ESG companies can attract more customers, as people increasingly buy from businesses they want to support.
- You can have a small impact on how easy it is for companies to raise funds in the future to support new projects.
- You'll likely still achieve good returns over time if you're investing in a big basket of stocks.

But there are some downsides...

- Higher fees. The stricter your ethical filter, the more time, research and effort that's required for the fund provider to build and manage the portfolio.
- Lower performance. By owning less companies, you may miss some winners. When you add higher fees, this becomes a considerable drag on returns.
- By avoiding certain shares, it's debatable whether this actually impacts the 'less ethical' companies in any meaningful way.
- Investing ethically is not as simple as it seems. It's extremely nuanced and complex.

A Couple of Larger Issues

Who's to say whether a company is ethical or not? Are tech companies unethical because they harvest our data? Are real estate developers unethical because they clear bushland to build houses? If green energy companies are ethical, what about the mining companies which provide them the materials to build green technology? You can't have one without the other.

If you avoid junk food and alcohol producers, do you avoid the supermarkets which sell it? If you avoid energy companies, what if they're also investing billions into green energy projects?

As you can see, it starts becoming incredibly intertwined and almost impossible to pry things apart. Every company is connected to every other company through its supply chain, logistics, and relationships. That's why slapping 'good' and 'bad' on a company is not that simple. If our goal is to hurt the 'unethical' companies, other ways are more effective.

How to Destroy Unethical Companies

Let's get one thing straight: companies don't receive our money when we buy shares. We're simply buying those shares from someone else in the marketplace. This means *not buying* certain shares doesn't actually hurt a company. Its sales, customers and profits remain the same. And profits are what keeps a company in business.

People banning together to avoid certain shares may result in a lower share price than otherwise. But this simply creates an opportunity for active investors to come in and scoop up cheap shares.

The reason these unethical companies stick around is not because people are buying their shares, *it's because people are buying their products.* To really hurt the company, you need to hurt its profits. And you do that in a couple of ways:

- Through society changing its shopping and lifestyle choices.
- Through putting pressure on governments to create incentives for new technologies and to regulate/restrict/tax harmful activities.

Our behaviours and lifestyle choices are at the core of the change we want to see. There's no point hating on fossil fuel companies while driving around in a petrol SUV and using coal-powered electricity at home. And no point complaining about land clearing, animal welfare, or the environment while munching on a beef burger and sipping a dairy-milk latte.

"But I want to use my money ethically, it's not about returns."

By accepting a lower long term return from ethical investing (very likely), it means we have *less money* to direct towards the stuff we really care about.

So, if you want to have the biggest per-dollar impact, I believe you should do that by investing in a normal index fund, and diverting the surplus returns or our spare personal cash to directly fund causes, charities, and organisations who are making a difference. This will have the most immediate and tangible impact, rather than hoping something will happen simply by avoiding certain shares.

"But isn't ethical investing better than nothing?"

I'm not suggesting you do nothing. I'm suggesting you choose an action which creates more tangible real-world results. Here's an example:

You have $1 million of shares invested in ESG funds. Because of higher fees and the likelihood of lower performance, you can perhaps expect your portfolio to return about 0.5% per year less than a typical index approach. That amounts to $5,000 per year. You could hope that this somehow makes a marginal difference.

Or you could instead invest in a regular index fund, make $5,000 more return, then use this to buy solar panels for yourself, a family member, a friend – hell, even your neighbour! If you did this every year, after a while your whole street will be completely solar powered. You are making an immediate reduction to fossil fuel profits, supporting green technology by buying the panels, *and* doing something wonderful for the community.

You can apply this principle to whichever ethical cause you care about the most. In my view, this is how you make a real difference and change the world!

Don't get me wrong, ethical investing comes from a wonderful place. But there is too much politics and posturing involved, and not enough tangible impact. It's not the magic solution to the world's problems that it's marketed to be. Invest this way if it's what you feel best about, not because of promises of high returns or changing the world.

Picking Your Own Stocks

Some people love the idea of choosing which companies to invest in. The main appeal of stock picking is the chance that some of your chosen companies do amazingly well, and you make a fortune.

Possible? Yes. Likely? Mmm, not really. Like many people, I've picked stocks myself in the past, with mixed results. Some companies powered along and zoomed up in price more than 100%. Of course, I attributed this to my genius and foresight. Others ran into problems, and I often lost 50% or more, which was naturally put down to bad luck!

In all seriousness, picking stocks can be a roller-coaster ride. Your results will be far more volatile and it's not easy to stick with. The embarrassing truth is, I would have had similar or better results doing nothing and instead putting my money in an index fund. The main reason I stopped was actually not due to performance, but to make my investing simpler, more hands off, and to reclaim mental space and time to focus on other things.

Even if you do well picking stocks, you'll spend a surprising amount of time thinking about your companies, following or researching others, as well as checking and managing your portfolio. This extra commitment should be considered, yet it rarely is.

Sure, successful companies often have many traits in common. But it's not easy to know the next Amazon or Tesla in advance. If it was, everyone would do it!

By all means, if you feel you need to scratch this itch, go ahead. But make sure it's only a small part of your portfolio. Because the truth is, on average, you're better off with the boring approach I've already outlined.

Investing in 'Themes'

There are also countless numbers of ETFs which let you bet on a theme: electric cars, robotics, cybersecurity, and so on. This sounds cool, but I'd advise caution. Look: you may be right about the future of a certain industry. But more likely than not, most people know the same things you do, and the price of the companies in that industry are *already higher* because of their bright future.

Trying to predict the future is completely unnecessary. Whatever 'theme' we feel passionate about, if we're correct, that will be reflected in the share prices of the companies in that industry. So if our chosen theme (battery technology, for example) is a big winner, those companies will become a bigger part of the index over time. You'll still benefit without the risk of a specific bet.

Again, allocating a small amount to personal 'picks' won't be a dealbreaker. But you're probably realising that I prefer to stick with the basic building blocks of a portfolio and not fluff around too much with other stuff.

How I Invest, and Why

In truth, I've tried a bit of everything. Property investing, stock picking, active funds, and index funds.

In the early days, I was attracted to the idea of maximising returns at all costs, so I didn't mind taking extra risk with leverage or picking stocks. These days, I know a lot more about how wealth, mindset, and personal finance are all linked. While I still want to achieve good returns, my approach to investing can now be summed up like this:

Achieve the best possible return with the lowest amount of effort and stress.

This implies a balance. I want a good return, not just on my money, but on the time I've spent to earn that return. And I want to balance that goal with the desire for simplicity and peace of mind.

As I write this, my investment dollars go into a small number of things. Most goes into a couple of simple index funds. I also own one LIC and two real estate trusts.

I'm happy with this portfolio and I basically do nothing except collect the income from these assets. I spend very little time on my investments and simply buy more when I have spare cash. By the way, if I ever get sick of managing my own portfolio, I'd gladly put my money into a one-fund portfolio for ultimate simplicity.

Building Your Own Portfolio

Don't feel like you have to get it 'right' from the start. In fact, it's almost certain you'll tweak your strategy over time. Everyone does. And while I've shared some ideas, I can't tell you exactly what to invest in. I don't know what you're comfortable with, and what's important to you.

In this chapter, I've given you the key building blocks, so now it's about getting started with a simple approach that makes sense to you. But make sure most of your money is invested in a low-cost way that is highly diversified and easy to manage. The point of investing is that your money works for you, not the other way round.

Boring investing often creates exciting long-term results. But the opposite is rarely true.

While the investments I encourage may not seem thrilling, the life they help you build is nothing short of incredible.

It's also important to consider your spouse, if you have one. No point having an investment strategy which gets you all hyped-up, but confuses your partner. If something happens to you, this will create unnecessary stress for them. Plus, it's important to be on the same page and work towards your

STRONG MONEY AUSTRALIA

goals together. Could they handle your investments if you were no longer around?

This is a good reminder not to overcomplicate things. And it's one of the reasons I invest the way I do. If something happens to me, my partner doesn't have to do anything. A decent amount of passive income will continue to hit the bank account whether I'm here or not.

The Bottom Line

Focus on buying assets you can own forever, where you can be confident that they'll still be profitable in 50 years' time. And when you think it through, nothing can provide that level of comfort and certainty quite like diversified index funds.

Remember the big basic bet we're making by investing in shares: that the Australian and global economy does well over our lifetimes. That innovation and advances in technology keep making society wealthier, and that companies continue to grow more profitable over time.

As veteran Aussie investor Peter Thornhill once described the share market to me: *"It reflects the endeavours of the human race. If you believe that human endeavour will come to an end, then you could consider investing in something else, but I'm buggered if I can think of what will replace it."*

How to Get Started

Getting started is extremely simple. All you need to do is open a low-cost brokerage account (those fees add up too). I use Pearler, but there are many others like SelfWealth, Stake and CMC Markets. After this, you can get ready to buy your first shares.

Once you've decided what you want to invest in, make a habit of investing

196

regularly. I think every month is ideal. This creates momentum, keeps your motivation high, and gives you something exciting to look forward to each month.

Another powerful mindset shift is to treat your investing like you would any other bill. For example, pretend it's a mortgage.

Make investing a non-negotiable monthly commitment. A commitment to your wealth, and to your freedom.

Your monthly spending comes *after* this. To take it a step further, you can also automate your savings by setting up a regular transfer into your brokerage account, or by using a broker which offers automated investing (like Pearler). This allows you to automatically save and invest into a diversified portfolio on a schedule and dollar amount that works for you.

(If you'd like to be walked through how to buy your first shares and handle the admin side of things, check out the step-by-step guide on the book resources page. The guide also has screenshots, FAQs and how to automate your investments.)

I'd also encourage you to slowly increase your investment amounts over time. For example, if you're following a budget, bucketing, or a 'save-first' approach, aim to bump up the amount you set aside for investing each month, even by $10 or $20.

You won't even notice it. See how many times you can pull this trick. As time goes on, you'll get used to having slightly less spending money and will be investing more than you initially thought possible. And if you're following the 'mindful spending' approach, simply sweep all surplus dollars across to your investment account each month to buy more shares of your chosen funds. Every dollar counts!

The aim of this chapter is to give you the knowledge and the confidence to get started with shares. I hope that building a portfolio for lifetime wealth and passive income now feels a lot simpler and less stressful.

But we're not done yet. Next, I want to share with you the key investment principles to keep you on the right track as you work towards financial independence.

10

Investment Principles for Long Term Success

"The key to making money in stocks is not to get scared out of them." - *Peter Lynch*

You now know how to invest in a simple and effective way. But having well-selected investments is not enough. That's because it's our behaviour that helps maximise our long term results and avoid costly mistakes.

It took me a while to learn the lessons in this chapter. But as I came to realise their power, they've steadily helped improve my own investing, and I think they'll help you too.

Simplicity

This is the first rule for a reason. Many highly paid and intelligent people make investing seem more complex than it is. Sometimes it's because their livelihood depends on us thinking we need their help to invest well. But that's just not true.

At first, investing feels intimidating. But when we understand key concepts and follow sensible principles, we can take control of our finances and invest confidently without the need for high-paid helpers. After all, nobody cares about your wealth more than you.

Keeping your investments simple creates a long list of benefits, including:

- Less up-front research needed, so you can get started sooner.
- Easier to follow and manage, helping you stick to the plan.
- Less time required, which you can spend on more valuable things (hobbies, family, free time).
- Less decisions to make or things to worry about.
- Easier to get your spouse on board so you both understand what's happening.
- Higher likelihood of long-term success due to the above factors.

Not only that, but there's no reason to believe a more complicated strategy will perform any better. In fact, the opposite is true. Investing in shares is one of the few examples where less effort tends to create a better result.

Some people find this hard to believe and are drawn to complexity, thinking it must be smarter or more effective. But as Warren Buffett explains, *"there seems to be some perverse human characteristic that likes to make easy things difficult."*

Interestingly, Buffett is probably the most successful investor of all time. And he simply suggests that most people are best served by investing regularly into low cost index funds.

Compound Interest

We discussed earlier the mind-blowing example of how a single $1,000 investment can turn into $1,000,000 over a lifetime. But imagine when you're investing $1,000 a month, or $1,000 even each week.

Our takeaway, of course, is to start investing as soon as possible. The biggest mistake people make is waiting until they think they've figured it all out. Once you have some basic knowledge – this book is more than enough – you can get started and just learn more from experience.

To paraphrase financial writer Morgan Housel, Warren Buffett's magic is not that he's the world's greatest investor. It's that he's the world's *longest investor,* having invested for more than 80 years. Almost all of Buffett's wealth has come in the last few decades. This sounds like a miscalculation until you remember how compound interest works:

- Year 0: $1,000
- Year 10: $2,000
- Year 20: $4,000
- Year 30: $8,000
- Year 40: $16,000
- Year 50: $32,000
- Year 60: $64,000
- Year 70: $128,000
- Year 80: $256,000
- Year 90: $512,000
- Year 100: $1,024,000

Whether you want to retire extremely early or not, do your future self a big favour and start investing right now in cashflow-producing assets you can own forever.

Fees Matter

Just like returns, fees also compound over time. The tricky part is that investment fees sound so small. 1% seems harmless, right? Besides, we don't even notice these fees since they are automatically deducted from the value of our funds. But think of it this way: if you earn a return of 7% per year, then paying 1% means around 15% of your total return is gobbled up by fees.

Say $100,000 is invested for 30 years and earns 7% per year, before fees. A fund charging 1% per year in fees leaves you with a final balance of $564,000. A fund charging 0.2% per year leaves you with $716,000. The higher cost fund leaves you with 20% *less wealth* after 30 years. The lesson? Make sure the bulk of your investments are in low-cost funds.

Invest Regularly, and Don't Time the Market

Adding to your portfolio on a regular basis, also known as dollar-cost averaging, achieves the following:

- Reinforces your commitment to your future wealth.
- Creates momentum as you regularly see your portfolio getting bigger.
- Provides you with further motivation as this becomes a self-reinforcing loop.
- Takes your mind off the question, "when is the right time to invest?"

Seeing your progress each month gives you something to look forward to. Every time you invest, you now own more shares, which means larger future dividends.

The most damaging behaviour I see is when people try to figure out what the market will do next, so they can invest at the best possible time. Not only is this impossibly hard to do but people tie themselves up in knots. This ends up consuming an unhealthy amount of their energy and thoughts.

Timing the market sounds great in theory, but it's psychological torture. You're better served investing consistently: rain, hail, or shine. It's the most reliable way (one could argue, the ONLY way) to make progress towards financial independence. If you think you might fall prey to this, then strongly consider automating your investing to take the emotion out of it.

The market will go up and down. But over time, your purchase prices will average out. We can only know in hindsight when the best time to buy was. As famed investor Peter Lynch once put it: *"More money has been lost by investors trying to anticipate market corrections, than in the corrections themselves."*

What he's pointing out here is the 'opportunity cost' of not being invested, since most years see the market continue to pay dividends and increase in value.

Be a Happy Investor

As I see it, there are two main groups of investors. The first group is never happy regardless of what the market is doing:

- Market goes up = *"Prices are too high, everything's overvalued."*
- Market goes down = *"Arrgh, I'm losing money!"*
- Market goes nowhere = *"This sucks, what's the point of investing?"*

On the other hand, the second group of investors is always happy:

- Market goes up = *"Nice – I'm a little bit richer than before"*
- Market goes down = *"Yes, now I can buy even more at lower prices!"*
- Market goes nowhere = *"All good, I'll just sit back and watch my dividends roll in."*

Which type of investor would you rather be? We can choose to see the negative or the positive. The truth is that investments are unpredictable. We need to accept that. If everything was breezy and only good things happened, there would be no risk. And if there's no risk, there's no reward.

Shares provide higher returns over the long term precisely because of the risk and uncertainty we deal with in the short term.

In other words, we have to *earn* those long-term returns. And the way we do that is by adopting a healthy mindset through the uncertainty. By being a happy investor.

Diversify

Diversification sounds boring. But it's useful to spread our money across different investments. Here are four ways we can diversify, and why it helps:

Companies and sectors

By owning an index fund, you own a large group of businesses in all sorts of industries. Each sector has its ups and downs, so one sector may be struggling, while others are thriving. You're not reliant on one industry doing well.

Countries and economies

By investing in a global fund, you benefit from the growth of international companies and the unique strengths of other economies and industries that are not well represented in Australia, like technology giants and multinational consumer brands. Plus, this way all your investments aren't reliant on one country doing well forever.

Time

By investing each month, we're buying shares at different prices and in different market environments. This dollar-cost averaging is fantastic because it helps 'average' out our purchases. As the market rises, our money buys less shares, and as prices fall our money stretches further and buys more shares. In this way, you are effortlessly timing the market, without the stress. How cool is that?

Assets

We can also benefit by spreading our money between assets. Aussie shares, global shares, real estate trusts, residential property, cash, bonds, peer-to-peer lending, and more. The options are endless. If we own multiple assets, some will be doing better than others. This gives us more opportunities to buy assets which are offering good value.

These factors combine to ensure we get a smoother outcome by protecting against things that could work against us.

Be an Owner, Not a Trader

By owning shares, we're piggy-backing on the success of businesses. We benefit from their returns for as long as we own those shares.

Innovation, human endeavour, technology, and the increasing prosperity of the world is reflected in the share market over time. While prices can move all over the place, we need to remember what's really happening behind the scenes.

We own a slice of hundreds (even thousands) of businesses. Every day, thousands (even millions) of employees go to work, solve problems, generate ideas, create new products, and serve their customers. All this effort leads to higher earnings and bigger dividends for us shareholders.

The share price moves of Coles or ANZ today mean absolutely nothing. Did their business really change this week? Or did people simply keep shopping at Coles and paying their mortgage? Likewise for US companies. Are people still using their Apple iPhones and searching on Google? Most likely.

Forget about fluctuating prices. Over time, the share price follows the success (or otherwise) of each business. And your fund will reflect the success of the big basket of businesses inside it.

What's wrong with trading? Well, trading means you'll be buying and selling frequently. That comes with a few problems:

- More decisions to make.
- More brokerage costs.
- More capital gains taxes.
- More administration.
- More time spent managing and thinking about your portfolio.
- More stress.
- More chances of making poor decisions.
- Less freedom due to above (financial, mental, and time).

Traders nearly always underperform a buy-and-hold investor. They also disrupt the magic of compounding. To be clear, I'm not saying never adjust your investments (everyone does sometimes), but be mindful and consider any taxes and trade-offs before you do it.

Another key difference is that traders think about short-term price movements. Owners think about long-term value creation. Charts, news, prices, forecasts, and chatter are all a distraction to the true investor with an ownership mentality.

The investor cares about the businesses they own and the earnings they produce. That's what drives real world results in the end. So don't think in terms of 1, 2 or even 5 years. Think in terms of 10, 20, and 50 years.

Add a zero to your timeframe and you'll end up adding zeros to your wealth.

Expect a Bumpy Ride and Ignore the Noise

Markets are volatile. You will often see the value of your portfolio drop, and it won't feel good. There's always a crash coming. We just don't know when.

Don't be surprised when it eventually happens. If anything, you should expect unexpected events to occur. Big crashes (say, a 50% fall) are rare, but chances are you will experience one at some point. The challenge is staying the course. Because when the market is falling, there are endless predictions of how much worse things are going to get.

> "The stock market is the only market where things go on sale and all the customers run out of the store." - *Cullen Roche*

This happened during the Corona Crash in 2020, every panic before that, and it'll happen in the future too. People crave certainty, so we ask the experts what the markets will do next. They have no idea, of course, but they're asked for their best guess, so they give it. And to the relentlessly negative media, a market crash is like Christmas, because fear sells.

But for our goal of financial independence, all that matters is increasing our ownership stake to fund our freedom.

Despite the uncertainty, the investors who keep buying all the way down, and all the way back up (as the market recovers) are the biggest winners. Not because they outsmart everyone else, but because they deliberately avoid trying to be too clever, and simply keep investing.

Even during good times, you'll hear that "markets are set to fall", "good times are about to end", and so on. My advice? Ignore it. Look at any long-term stock market chart and you'll quickly decide that you wish you bought as much as possible, as early as possible, and that any fall is an opportunity.

The 120-year chart below shows how the Aussie market has multiplied more than 500 times in price appreciation alone. This doesn't even include the juicy dividends paid every single year along the way!

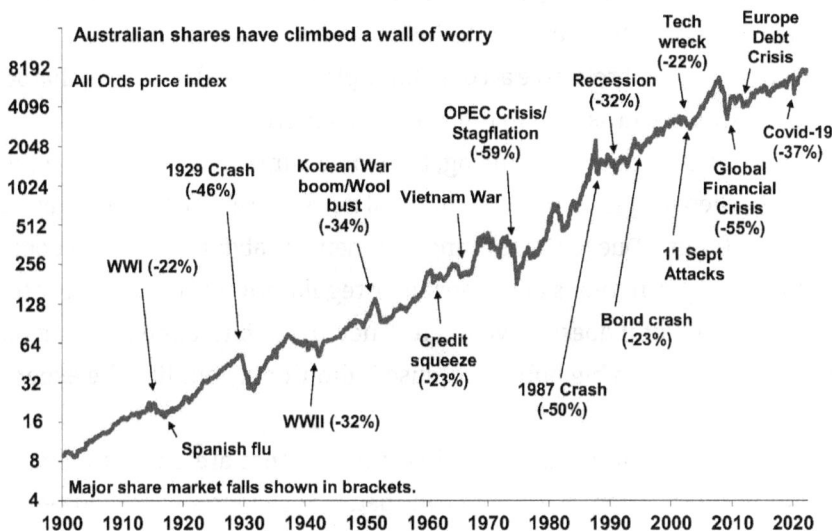

Source: ASX, AMP Capital

Switch your focus from days to decades and you'll become a more successful (and calmer) investor.

By the way, if you're a saver, lower share prices are exactly what you want. Experiencing big market falls while you're on your way to FI can actually juice your progress.

You get to do a lot of buying when prices are low, which gives you greater returns as the market eventually recovers. So, when the market is in a slump, ignore the negative news and stick to your plan.

Your Money Works for You, Not the Other Way Round

One common mistake is spending too much time focused on your investments. As a long-term owner, there's no need to constantly read about markets, check our brokerage account multiple times per day, or work harder to improve our returns. Often, this impedes our progress.

The smarter we *think* we're being, the worse our results. A good example of this is when people read all the financial news to feel like they're 'staying on top of things'. Due to the running commentary about impending doom, the investor gets nervous and stops their regular investing to wait for the promised fall. But it doesn't eventuate. They're left bitter and thinking the market must be in a big bubble because it didn't play out like the experts said.

There's simply no need to find investments that are going to give us gigantic returns. After all, are you really better at picking stocks than people who do it for a living? Probably not. But the good news is that you don't have to be, because your goals are different.

Always consider not just the return on your money, but on the time you spent to earn that return. Simple investments can give attractive long-term results with almost no effort.

Even if you can beat the market (unlikely), spending hours every week on your investments quickly becomes another job. Unless you truly find it meaningful, this time is better spent elsewhere. Your money works for you, not the other way round. And it doesn't work harder when you're watching it!

Focus on What You Can Control

The best way to approach investing (and life) is to focus on the things we can control. Not only does this make your experience more enjoyable and less stressful, but it's a more effective use of energy.

When it comes to investing, there are no guaranteed outcomes. So, what do we have control over? Here's a few things:

- How much you put aside for investing each month.
- Investing on a regular basis no matter what.
- Which funds you choose to invest in (simple, diversified, low cost).
- Ignoring the noise and keeping your goals in mind.
- Reinvesting your dividends.
- Focus on increasing your ownership of income producing assets.

If you want your investments to grow faster, simply put more money into your portfolio.

Your input (how much savings you add) is far more important than the output (your investment returns).

Compound interest shows that earning massive returns from investments comes long after the saving has been done. Not many people mention that because it's sexier to talk about fast gains. But as we saw in chapter three, the bulk of your portfolio (and whether you reach FI in 10 or 15 years) will largely be determined by your savings rate.

Don't Chase Performance

People can make tons of money with all sorts of things in the short term (speculative stocks, trading crypto, using options, etc.). But over the long run, nearly everyone will struggle to beat a buy-and-hold approach. If you want to choose some separate investments on the side, that's fine. But focus most of your money on your 'boring' long term portfolio, as this will fund your freedom. Your future is too important to rely on lotto tickets.

There's also a tendency for new investors to look for investments that have recently performed the best and park their money there. But that's usually a bad idea. The performance of different assets and markets tends to even out over time. Basically, nothing outperforms forever. This year's top performer may be overtaken by something else next year.

For example, from 2010-2020, the US share market returned 16.8% per annum. That's nearly double the long-term average. By comparison, the Aussie share market returned 8.3% per annum.

Clearly, US shares are a better investment, right? Not so fast. Let's look back a little further. In the previous decade (2000-2010), US shares returned -4.3% per annum. Yes, negative returns. On the other hand, Aussie shares returned 10.3% per annum.

This gives us two lessons:

- Markets can go through very strong and very poor periods.
- Start and end dates have a huge influence on how good an investment looks.

For completeness: since 1900, the US and Aussie markets have performed about the same (10% per annum), each having periods of outperformance and underperformance.

The Power of Dividends

Dividends are one of the greatest *and* most underappreciated parts of investing in shares:

- Dividends are an effortless income stream which grows over time.
- Dividends help you focus on the big picture: owning profitable, cash-generating businesses.
- Dividends give you regular cash to reinvest into more shares or rebalance your portfolio without selling.
- Dividends are a source of return that's not reliant on the market's mood.

- Dividends serve as regular positive feedback that you're doing the right thing.

Let me expand on these points.

Each year companies announce how much profit they've made. Most companies pass on a chunk of this profit to shareholders in the form of dividend payments. The rest is reinvested into the business.

This is also the case for investors in diversified share funds, too. We're investing in a big basket of companies, most of which pay dividends, and this cash is passed on to us every 3-6 months depending on the fund.

Here's the cool part: dividends are based on profits, not share prices. This means your dividend income is reliant on the underlying businesses, not whether the share market is up or down. This reminds us exactly what's happening behind the scenes: companies working hard to provide products and services, generating profits for shareholders.

Of course, when profits fall during a recession, dividends drop too. But we'll *still* receive a positive stream of income every year, even if we have no clue what prices will do. This acts as a source of comfort, especially during downturns. People who shrug their shoulders at dividends usually underappreciate this behavioural aspect which is helpful for a lot of people. By focusing on the dividends our investments are providing, we can sit back and enjoy the income stream, rather than constantly fret about the prices, which is what brings so many people unstuck in the share market.

Most importantly, since companies grow their profits over time, that means dividends get bigger, too. Which, by the way, is exactly why the share market rises. Higher earnings and dividends mean companies are more valuable. As John Bogle summarised it:

> "Successful investing is about owning businesses and reaping the huge rewards provided by the dividends and earnings growth of our nation's – and, for that matter, the world's – corporations."

Dividend Dates

Having those dividends hit the bank account each quarter is also a great thing to see as a newbie, or possibly even to show your spouse, who may not be quite as comfortable investing in shares. Remember: as you invest more, those payments get bigger and bigger.

You could even celebrate each quarter by going on 'Dividend Dates' where you head out for lunch or a coffee as a little reward for your consistent efforts to save and invest. Besides, it's also a great reminder to take time out and chat about how your finances are going.

If you're single, you can reward yourself for growing your wealth and passive income in the same way. Or get a mate on board and you can discuss your journey together over a tasty beverage.

For many of us, looking at the income stream from our shares makes it feel more real. After all, this is tangible proof you are getting real passive income, from real companies, with real employees.

Compounding Dividends

Now, people often think, *"but dividends are so small, surely they're not big enough to matter."* And sure, they aren't massive. Dividends from a diversified portfolio are often in the range of 3-4% per year. But you might be surprised at the impact of dividends over time.

From 1970 to 2020, the S&P 500 returned 4,003% in capital gains. Pretty impressive. **But if all dividends were reinvested, the total return was 16,885%. That's more than 4x greater!**

Over this period, roughly 76% of the investor's return came from receiving and reinvesting their dividends. How incredible is that? As a long-term investor, using your dividends to buy more shares makes a huge difference to your wealth!

Now let's look at an example of someone investing for FI over 15 years. If they're like many people and only care about the price of their shares, their investment would look like this...

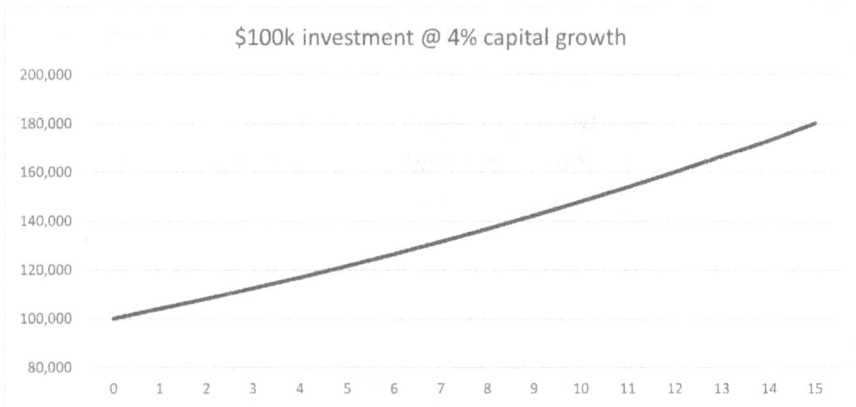

$100k investment @ 4% capital growth

An unexciting result, but not bad. The investor has almost doubled their money, turning $100,000 into $180,000. But we haven't included dividends, so let's do that now. We'll assume yearly dividends of 4%.

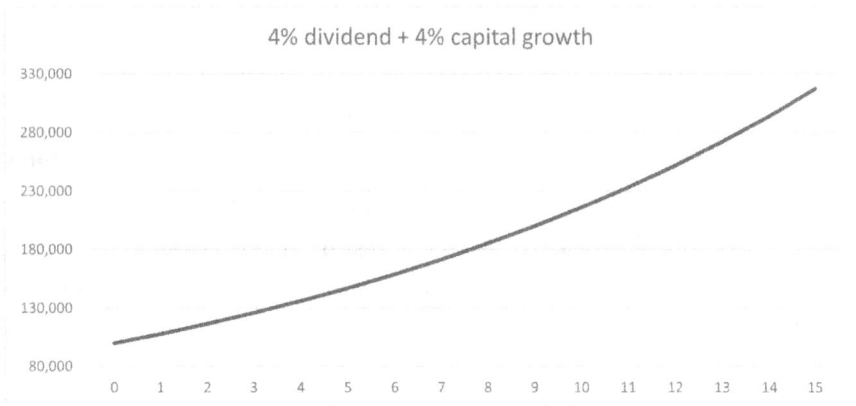

4% dividend + 4% capital growth

Now we're getting somewhere. The $100,000 has more than tripled to $317,000. Again, we see the power of reinvesting dividends. By the way, you can choose to have your dividends reinvested automatically via a dividend reinvestment plan (DRP), or receive that money in your account and add it to your next purchase. It doesn't matter which one you choose. What matters is that when you're accumulating, you *always* use your dividends to buy more shares.

But even this is a poor example. If you're pursuing FI, your progress will look radically different to this.

Because you're not investing once and leaving it alone. You are constantly saving and adding to your investments. Rather than leave that lump of cash to work by itself, let's see what happens when we add $40,000 to our investments each year.

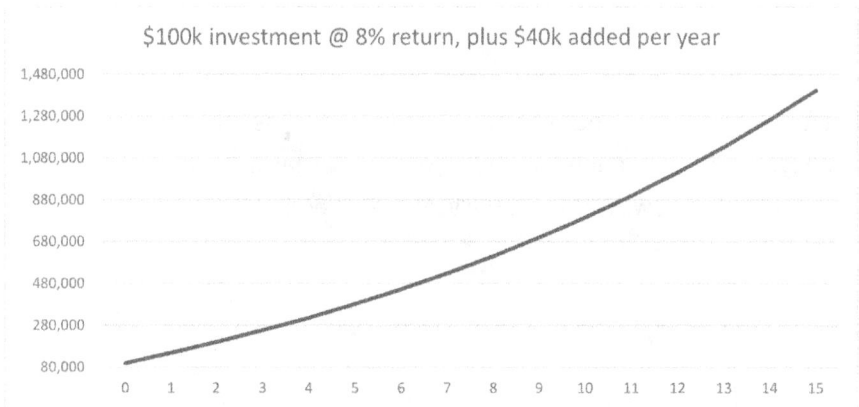

$100k investment @ 8% return, plus $40k added per year

Ahh, here we go! The end balance after 15 years is around $1.4 million, producing a passive income of $56,000 per year. What a difference regular saving makes! And to be clear, even if you start at zero, the end balance is still more than $1 million. Of course, your progress won't be a straight line like this, but you get the idea. Now let's compare all three examples.

Share Price vs Accumulation vs Accumultion with Extra Investment

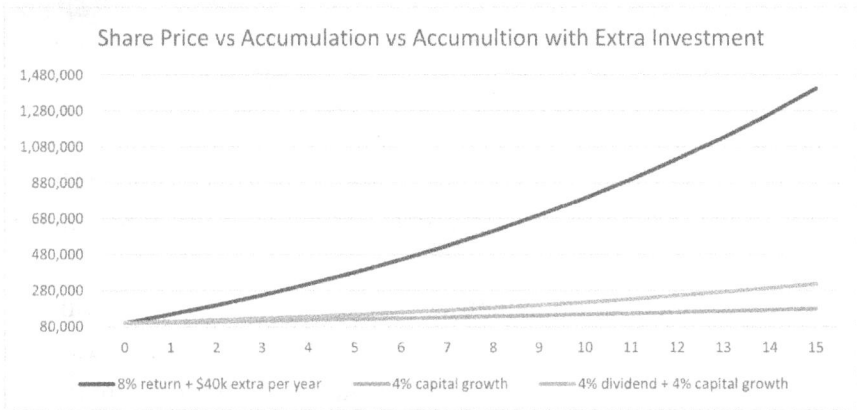

As you can see, most of the progress is created by adding savings to the portfolio, just like we showed in chapter three. This means that even in a slow-moving share market, you'll still be making massive progress.

I have to warn you about something: receiving dividends for 'doing nothing' will feel magical. It may even become addictive. As you invest and use your dividends to buy even more shares, your passive income snowball starts to build momentum. Here's what happens:

· Every single time you buy shares, your dividend income gets bigger.
· Every time you reinvest your dividends, your dividend income gets bigger.
· Every time companies increase their dividends, your dividend income gets bigger.

When any of these things occur, your passive income grows and your financial position becomes stronger. If that's not motivating, I don't know what is!

Boosting Returns vs Boosting Savings

Learning and optimising along the way to financial freedom is key. But we also need to know where our efforts are most rewarded. I mentioned how a simple approach is best and that we probably shouldn't try to chase higher returns. But let's say you try anyway. Is it worth your time?

Spending 5 hours a week finding better investments or outsmarting the market *could* prove fruitful. But more than likely, it won't. In contrast, even 1 hour a week spent optimising your lifestyle, expenses, or earning more income will be very well rewarded.

By using the mindset and principles in this book, it's easy to imagine turning a 15% savings rate into 45%. That's triple the result. Now, you might be clever, but I'm telling you that turning a long-term return of 8% per year into 24% per year is not going to happen!

Even Warren Buffett (arguably the world's greatest investor) has achieved returns of 'only' around 20% per year.

Too many people waste precious time and mental energy trying to juice returns when they could make much more progress with a few other tweaks.

Adding to your investments is far more achievable, repeatable, and reliable than adding to your returns.

Investors chasing high returns are often trying to 'out-earn' their spending habits. Just like a binge-eater tries to 'out-train' their poor nutrition with hardcore exercise. Unfortunately, we can't control investment returns. On the other hand, we have much more control over our income and spending.

Financial independence is more reliant on your ability to save than to make genius investing moves. It's not how much you make, but how much you keep.

Investing is like planting a tree. If we leave it alone, it will grow okay by itself. But if we feed it (add savings), the tree will grow faster and deliver more fruit (dividends). We plant the tree once and can harvest the fruit forever. Hell, we can even cut off a few branches if we need to (sell shares) and the tree will regrow these over time.

At this point, my message is clear: invest as much as you can, as soon as you can, into simple diversified investments like low-cost index funds. Still, you might be wondering: "but what if I have a lump sum, like a big bonus, inheritance, or stockpile of savings?"

How to Invest a Lump Sum

Here's where it gets a little tricky. Because markets deliver positive returns most years, the winning play tends to be investing a lump sum all at once. And for an experienced investor, that's probably the right move. But for a beginner, I think it's better to invest a lump sum over time for multiple reasons:

- You get used to the price movements and seeing your investment fluctuate.
- Your purchases will even out, buying some at lower prices and some higher.
- You reduce the chance of a poor outcome by going 'all-in' at one point in time.
- You're still learning so it's best to start with as little stress as possible.

On average, dumping a lump sum into the market is the most profitable approach. Remember, it's *time in* the market, rather than *timing* the market. But sometimes it's not, and those times can be painful. This may lead to regret and feeling like you made a mistake.

On the other hand, dollar cost averaging over 12 months (for example) is far easier psychologically. Investing $10,000 per month for 15 months is much less stressful than investing $150,000 in one hit! If prices go up, you feel fine. And if prices go down, you can be excited to scoop up more shares next month at a lower price.

In reality, there are pros and cons to both approaches. Another method is to invest one lump immediately (say, half) and dollar cost average the rest. This helps avoid regret of choosing the wrong approach since you're essentially choosing both. In conclusion: there's no right answer, so do what you feel most comfortable with.

Summary

We've covered a lot in this chapter. Here's a short summary:

- Choose a simple investment strategy you can stick with.
- Invest as soon as possible to make the most of compound interest.
- Fees matter. Make sure the bulk (if not all) of your investments are low cost.
- Invest on a regular schedule (like monthly) and avoid trying to time the market.
- Diversify to avoid the chance of a poor long-term outcome.
- Be a long-term owner of income producing assets, not a twitchy short-term trader.
- Expect volatility, handle it like a stoic, and ignore the gloomy news.
- Stay focused on what you can control, like saving and investing regularly.
- Reinvest your dividends and watch your passive income snowball grow.
- To juice progress, increase your savings rather than chasing returns.

You don't build a large portfolio by watching and waiting, analysing and procrastinating, or making a few perfectly timed purchases. You get there by investing as much as you can, whenever you can, for as long as you can.

Ignore the noise and keep increasing your ownership of income producing assets.

I trust these lessons will help you navigate the markets for many years to come. Be sure to come back to this section at any point in the future should you need a refresher.

Now let's turn our focus to some other important financial topics: superannuation and mortgages. We'll also discuss how to enjoy the journey, staying motivated, and some final optimisations.

11

Super, Mortgages, and Enjoying the Journey

"I'm too busy working on my own grass to notice if yours is greener." - *Unknown*

We've talked a lot about how to build a great long term investment portfolio. But we haven't discussed one of the biggest assets most Aussies will build during their lives: superannuation.

How does super even fit into your strategy when your goal is to be financially independent in your 30s or 40s? Should you include it in your plans? Do you forget about it? Is it wise to invest more into super or simply leave it alone?

These factors depend on many things:

- The age you plan to reach FI.
- How much super you expect to have.
- Whether you'll have enough wealth outside super to live on.
- And how you feel about the superannuation system in general.

But regardless of your thoughts on it, super deserves our attention since it's likely to become an important part of our wealth over time.

How Much Does Super Matter?

For young adults today, the superannuation system will exist for their entire working careers. That's unlike previous generations. And while super feels tiny in the beginning, most people will end up with more upon retirement than they expect.

Take a 25-year-old with $20,000 in super. Let's assume they have an average full-time wage of $80,000, which grows with inflation throughout their career, and that their super returns 5% after inflation. At age 65, they'll end up with $1,107,198 in today's dollars.

We're assuming no real income growth and that super contributions don't rise to 12% from the 10% they are in 2022. Pretty conservative. Put simply: it's going to be a large amount of money.

> "OK great, but how does super fit with my financial independence plans?"

There's a couple of approaches. Some people like to invest as much as possible into super because of the tax benefits. Others don't put a single extra dollar into super and build up their personal investments instead. Let's discuss both.

Going All-in on Super:

PROS:

- You can get a tax deduction for adding extra to super (with limits).

- Super investments are taxed at low rates: 15% for income and 10% for long term capital gains. That's much lower than investments in your personal name.
- No extra accounts or investments to manage since super is already set up.

CONS:

- Your money isn't accessible until age 60. It's hard to retire early without access to savings and investments!
- Rules can be changed at any time, including taxes, limits, and the access age.
- If you're investing inside and outside super, you need to make sure your personal portfolio is big enough to last until you can access super. That can be tricky to balance, and given the above, your plans are more vulnerable and less within your control.

Investing Outside Super:

PROS:

- Complete control over what to invest in.
- Access to the income and value of your investments at any time.
- Helps you create freedom to retire earlier.
- Super is still compounding in the background for you to access later.

CONS:

- Pay a higher tax on investments compared to investing extra into super.
- Miss out on the tax deductions for adding to super.
- Miss out on extra wealth and higher returns due to the above.

Personally, adding to super was not part of my FIRE plans.

I'd rather pay more tax and have access to the money now, than get a tax deduction by locking up my money for another 30 years. Would you rather have $1 million you can access, or $3 million you can't? Which one lets you build your best possible life while you're young and healthy enough to enjoy it? All the tax savings in the world weren't going to help you become financially independent. Far better to be wealthy and free in your 30s, than work until you're filthy rich in your 60s.

Having said that, adding extra to super can make sense for some people.

When Super Is the Clear Winner

If you're starting this journey in your 40s or later, using the benefits of super is often a good idea. Depending on your savings rate and current situation, you may reach FI in 10-15 years anyway, which puts you close to super access age (usually 60).

In this case, you could divert a good chunk of your savings into super, since the tax benefits will maximise your nest egg, and it fits nicely with your timeframe. The specific details can become complex and are outside the scope of this book. So it's worth researching further or even getting advice in this area.

If you haven't started investing yet, there's a good chance super already makes up a decent part of your net worth. For this reason, it may be wise to also invest outside super so that you aren't reliant on the rules around super staying the same. While this may mean more tax, it also gives more options and control.

If you are in this age range and have a decent super balance already, you could even consider semi-retirement. By that I mean you go into cruise mode until you hit your super access age. There are many cases where a single person or family could have a paid-off home and a reasonable super balance by age 40-50. They could easily move to part-time work, enjoy more freedom now and maybe even invest a little on the side while their super continues to grow in the background.

If you're flexible, open to working part-time, or willing to adjust your spending to make it work, there are countless scenarios where the average household can create a lot more freedom sooner than traditional retirement by using super as a later-stage strategy.

How Should Early Retirees Think about Super?

To live a free and independent life at a young age, you're best served by saving and investing outside super. This is the fastest way to make work optional.

Personally, I've always seen superannuation as 'bonus money' that serves as a handy backup plan and extra cushion for later. Not because I don't trust it. But because my goal was to be wealthy at a young age, thereby making super less critical to my plans. Don't get me wrong: super will remain an important part of your lifetime wealth. Even if you retire at 30 and never make another super contribution, your super will grow to a useful amount.

Let's say that you leave work at 30, live off your personal investments, and never work again (extremely unlikely, but stick with me). A super balance of $100,000 (left untouched with no money added) would grow to $400,000 by age 60 (after adjusting for inflation). That's good enough for a yearly passive income stream of probably $20,000. Very handy indeed!

As you can see, even these conservative numbers show that super matters. So how can we make the most of it?

Choosing a Good Super Fund

Most Aussies are invested in their super fund's 'default' option by, um, default. This is sometimes called a 'balanced' fund, which spreads your money between shares, infrastructure, property, and fixed interest like bonds and cash.

These default options are decent, but they're usually quite conservative. For example, many funds allocate 25% to bonds and cash, which make the portfolio less volatile. But this comes at a cost: lower long-term returns. It's almost like having a quarter of your money sitting in recliners sipping tea.

While it might seem prudent to reduce risk, it doesn't make sense to have so much tied up in low-risk, low-return investments if we aren't touching this money for another 30 years. So what do I suggest instead?

Firstly, stick with not-for-profit super funds, which have shown to be the lowest cost and best performing funds over the long term (those two things go together!). There are plenty of reputable super funds out there. A few examples are Australian Retirement Trust, Rest, and Hostplus.

And if you'd like your super to work a little harder over your lifetime, go for a more aggressive investment style. Two ways to do that are to select either the 'high growth' option, or allocate 100% to indexed shares, which many super funds offer. This should help maximise long-term returns and means less of our dollars are lounging around and taking it easy.

I've opted for this approach myself using the indexed shares option with Australian Retirement Trust. Extremely simple, low cost, and I'm confident it will have healthy performance.

Should we invest our super less aggressively after we retire? In many cases, reaching FI in our 30s, 40s, or even 50s means we still have many, many decades of investing ahead of us. That suggests that it's better to remain heavily invested in higher-returning assets. But it also depends on your plans for super, how and when you want to use it, and your risk tolerance. There's no right answer for everyone.

If you're young and want to reach FI as early as possible, focus on investing outside super for complete control, access, and flexibility. Every investment in your personal name brings you one step closer to freedom.

Set your super up for success with the above strategies and let it compound in the background. Even if you plan to retire early, it will serve as a nice additional pool of wealth for later in life.

Should You Pay Off Your Mortgage or Invest?

Some people pay off their mortgage before they get into investing. Others say, "forget the mortgage and focus on building your investments."

And some take the middle ground, doing a bit of both. So what should you do?

First up, here's the arguments for paying off your home loan:

- Paying down your mortgage is a tax-free guaranteed return, whereas investment returns fluctuate from year to year, and some tax is payable.
- You'll save a ton of money in interest over the life of your loan.
- You get to watch your debt go down every single month, which can be extremely motivating.
- A paid-off home greatly reduces your living expenses, forever. You then don't need as much in investments to live off.
- There are psychological benefits to being a debt-free homeowner. I'm yet to meet a person who doesn't speak fondly about having paid-off their home.

Why Investing Might Be Better

- You're likely to earn higher returns: maybe 6% per year after tax vs 3-4%.
- Your wealth will grow at a faster rate, possibly helping you reach FI faster.
- Investing diversifies your wealth by having money spread across different assets, rather than a single property.
- More control over your wealth. You can easily change your investments if your risk tolerance shifts or if you simply want to move money from one asset to another.

· Your savings are liquid. You can sell shares to create a lump of cash for any reason at any time. With a paid-off home, all that equity sits in your house and you usually can't access it (especially in retirement).

Does Debt Affect Our Ability to Retire Early?

You might be thinking, *"but if we want to be financially free, surely we need to pay off our mortgage! How can you leave work when you still have debt?"*

Debt by itself doesn't actually matter. As long as you have enough investments to meet your expenses, *you're fine.* Can you access enough cash from your investments to pay the bills? Congratulations, you don't have to work anymore!

On a personal note, we had plenty of debt upon leaving work. But it didn't matter because we always had access to cash to pay the bills. At this point, it's clear there are benefits to paying off your home *and* focusing on investments. So, should we do both?

The Double Goal Dilemma

As strange as it sounds, trying to do both things can be worse than focusing on one. Here's what I mean (we'll ignore compounding for simplicity):

Say you start with a $400,000 mortgage. Your interest rate is 3%, and repayments are $1,687 per month, or $20,244 per year. To tackle this, you make extra repayments on your loan to the tune of $200,000. At the same time, you also save hard and build a share portfolio of $200,000.

By all accounts, you've done a great job. You've built investments and reduced your debt. But despite putting in $200,000, your mortgage repayments remain the same. You'll simply become debt-free sooner.

The investments are paying \$8,000 in dividends per year (4%). But consider this: if you focused *solely* on your mortgage, that \$400,000 debt would now be gone. And that means no more mortgage repayments, leaving you with an extra \$20,244 per year. That's \$12,000 better than trying to do both.

Strategy	Money allocated	Cashflow improvement
Get rid of mortgage	\$400,000	\$20,244 per year
Investments only	\$400,000	\$16,000 per year
Half mortgage, half invest	\$200,000 + \$200,000	\$8,000 per year

What does this mean? Well, if your goal is to retire as early as possible, it's often better to either maximise your investments *or* smash your mortgage. This helps you reap the biggest rewards without getting stuck in the middle zone of having a half paid-off home which doesn't improve your cashflow.

If you're in this half-half situation, don't worry. You can usually ask your lender to recalculate your repayments if you've paid extra. This will improve your cashflow by reducing the monthly payment required.

Of course, you can time it so that your mortgage hits zero by the time you reach FI.

You do this by making enough extra repayments so that it lines up with your estimated timeframe to retirement. To help you fine tune this, you need an 'extra repayment' mortgage calculator and an FI calculator. You'll find both on the book resources page.

But that's only one mortgage strategy of many! Here's a few more options to consider...

Mortgage Strategies to Optimise Your Cashflow for FI

- **Strategy 1:** Pay off your mortgage as soon as possible. Focus every dollar here, then build investments.
- **Strategy 2:** Pay enough extra on the mortgage so it will be gone by the time you reach FI. Invest the rest.
- **Strategy 3:** Pay the bare minimum on your mortgage. Focus 100% on investing. Reach FI with your mortgage still being paid off over time from your investment income.
- **Strategy 4:** Same as strategy 3, but after leaving work (and entering a lower tax bracket), sell some shares to pay off the mortgage. Your money works harder this way, and leaves you with lower expenses when you retire.
- **Strategy 5:** Pay interest-only on your mortgage. Focus on investing. Any savings can be kept in an offset account which will reduce your monthly interest payment. This maximizes investments even more. Later, you can decide whether to pay off the loan or not. Keep in mind, the interest rate will probably be higher for this type of loan.
- **Strategy 6:** Make minimum mortgage repayments and focus on investing. Then, before leaving work, refinance to a new 30-year loan term (or as long as possible). You're aiming to make your mortgage payment as little as possible. This is possibly my favourite strategy of them all, because it almost feels like a magic trick...

As an example:

- Say you start with a 30-year loan of $400,000 at a 3% interest rate.
- Repayments are $1,687 per month, or $20,244 per year.
- After ten years of normal repayments, your loan balance will be around $300,000.
- Your repayments are still the same and there's 20 years left on the loan.
- Now you refinance to a fresh 30-year loan term.

· Your repayments now fall to $1,265 per month, or $15,180 per year.

The result? Your yearly cashflow improves by $5,000! That's like having an extra $125,000 in investments. Your expenses have fallen, so you now need less for FI. Your lifestyle is the same and your home is still being paid off. Of course, it will take longer to become debt free and you'll pay more interest overall. But your bills are lower, so you can retire earlier (or with less investments) due to the improved cashflow. Pretty cool, right?

These options give you more flexibility and control over your finances, and therefore your life. You can always switch between these strategies depending on your priorities at the time.

Just to be clear, I'm not actively encouraging you to never pay off your home. If you need the benefit of forced savings, or prefer the certainty of being mortgage-free, then smash that loan! But for those with strong financial discipline, good habits, and the desire to optimise, your cashflow and freedom can be improved using some of the other options.

There are two more financial strategies which some people use to accelerate the wealth-building process. Both are optional and not suitable for everyone, but I should at least mention them here.

Debt Recycling

Debt recycling aims to turn your current non-deductible home loan into a tax-deductible investment loan. In simple terms, you take money you were going to invest and pay down your home loan instead. Then, you pull that money back out using a separate loan and invest it into income-producing assets. In doing so, this part of the debt becomes tax deductible.

The result is you end up paying much less tax on your investment income. As you keep paying extra off your home loan, you continue to re-borrow that money to invest and build your portfolio. You can use the investment income and regular savings to pay down your non-deductible home loan even faster to speed up this process.

Now, there's a bit more to it than that and it must be structured correctly, but hopefully you get the idea. This strategy is mostly about saving on tax while investing. It can be effective, but it does add some complexity and extra work.

Borrowing to Invest

This strategy is about taking on more debt to grow your portfolio faster and (hopefully) increase your returns. Borrowing to invest can be powerful, but it adds risk and has no guarantee of paying off, depending on your investments and your timeframe.

If you can borrow at 3-4% and achieve a long-term return of 7-8%, it's easy to see why this can be popular. While borrowing to invest can build your wealth faster, there's plenty of extra risk and complexity to consider before diving in.

For the sake of simplicity, and the fact that neither of these strategies are necessary to reach FI, the details have been left out of this book. I have written in-depth articles on both topics on my blog, so I'll link to these articles on the book resources page if you'd like to learn more. But here's something worth remembering:

With a good savings rate, you don't need to use leverage to retire early or become very wealthy over time.

Taxes and the Bigger Picture

Don't worry too much about tax. Yes, I know, you already pay a fair chunk of tax. And guess what? As your investments grow and you become increasingly wealthy, you'll probably pay more. But that's the way it should be.

The easiest way to pay less tax is to make less money. Not so appealing, right? Besides, once you start living off your investments (or even semi-retire), your taxes will be pretty damn low. Let me explain.

Under the current Australian tax system, each person can receive around $20,000 in income before *any* tax is payable. For a couple, that's $40,000 per year, tax-free. But it gets better. Aussie share dividends come with franking credits (which count as tax paid on your behalf), reducing your tax bill or resulting in a tax refund. Plus, when you sell any shares, you only pay tax on the capital gain. And since you'll have owned your shares for longer than 12 months, you benefit from the Capital Gains Tax (CGT) discount, meaning only half your gain is taxable.

Overall, this means taxes on your portfolio and the cash you generate to live on will be *very* low. There's no need to assemble a team of hotshot lawyers and savvy tax specialists to re-route your money through a web of trusts and overseas bank accounts like some ridiculous game of Cayman Islands snakes and ladders.

Just keep it simple and relax. You're getting richer, so focus on that. Your time and mental energy are too precious to be wasted on mild annoyances. Remember: the ultimate goal is to make our financial affairs *effortless*.

In this book, we've flipped a number of things on their head. We're also doing that by turning money from a source of stress and worry into a source of freedom and contentment.

Our relationship with money can enslave us or empower us. Which one will it be?

Thoughts for Late Starters

Everyone's situation is different, but I have a few thoughts for those starting in their 40s and later. The choices you have on where to put your money are the same, but you may prioritise them differently. Here are some options...

Mortgage:

Getting rid of your mortgage (if you have one) lifts a weight off your shoulders. With much lower expenses, life becomes cruisy. This alone gives many people the confidence to be more selective about how much and what type of work they do.

Superannuation:

Because you can access it sooner, super is a more attractive home for your savings compared to younger readers. Even if you add nothing extra, it still may end up being more than you think. Say you're 45 now with $150,000 super. By age 65, this figure would likely be closer to $600,000 thanks to compounding returns. That's good enough for a yearly income stream of around $25,000.

Pension:

You'll have access to the pension upon traditional retirement age, unless you're wealthy by that point. This also serves as a handy and reliable source of income. Despite the scary stories, the pension is actually not that bad, and increases with inflation over time. It goes a long way to paying the bills, especially for those with other savings and/or paid-off housing. Be sure to account for this in your plans.

Investments:

If you already have (or will have) a decent super balance, you won't need as many investments outside super. If you can access a super income stream at age 60 (and the pension at 65–67), then in your 50s you only really need enough money to last you 10 years, which can be a blend of investment income and part-time work.

Using a combination of the above (investments, part-time work, being mortgage-free, superannuation, and the pension) there are plenty of ways to tweak the numbers to fund your lifestyle.

If your goal is to create freedom as soon as possible, I'd still focus on building investments outside super. This will immediately reduce your reliance on work income. And if you build decent wealth by your 50s, you can comfortably start living off this while your super grows in the background. Alternatively, you could also invest extra into super if you plan to live on part-time income until your super access age.

Now, I know these might seem like vague instructions. But that's because there's an infinite number of ways you could mix these moving parts to suit your own situation and goals.

For most late starters (like the rest of us), the fastest way to a level of independence is by either paying off the mortgage, building your investments, and combining that with some part-time work you enjoy. If you can maintain a small savings surplus, with super continuing to grow in the background, you've got the recipe for many happy decades of doing your own thing.

Having said all that: to reap the benefits, we must actually follow through and reach our destination. Sometimes, that's easier said than done, because there's a difficult hurdle known as the *Boring Middle*.

The 'Boring' Middle Part of Your FI Journey

Your financial adventure will start off extremely exciting. Dollars begin to pile up and you can see your future options expanding. At the other end, the late stage of your journey is equally exciting, filled with anticipation as you count down the days to freedom.

And then there's the middle.

You've got your finances running smoothly. You're saving and investing regularly. Now it's a case of repeating this winning recipe until your investments are big enough to live off forever. A waiting game, if you will. Hardly thrilling, is it?

The main problem with the 'boring' middle is that there's not much to do. You're already doing all the right things. You just wish it would go faster. Hurry up already, I want to be free! You might start to wonder if early retirement will ever come. Can you really wait another 5-10 years to reach this glorious state of freedom? After all, it feels sooo long.

I remember these feelings well. Here's my advice for getting through the boring middle, how I approached it, and what I'd do in that same position today.

Solution #1: Frame it Differently

When you have a burning desire to achieve a goal, it's normal to get impatient and want to skip to the end. But consider this: how incredible is it that financial independence is even possible?

We can actually get to the point where we control 100% of our time, all in just a decade or two. Ten years of hard work for a lifetime of freedom is an awesome deal. And you still get to live a good life along the way!

The opportunity itself is something to be grateful for. This simply wasn't possible for most of human history, until the huge increase in wealth and incomes over the last 100 years.

Some people express frustration about not finding out about FI sooner. But what if you never found out at all? Imagine you worked another 10, 20, or 30 years and never knew. Now *that* would be a real tragedy.

Being pleased about where we're headed is just as important as the actions we're taking. Focus on making the most of your *current life*, while slowly working towards your ideal life. Once you reach FI, you might even look back with fond, rose-tinted glasses on the years of hard work that built your incredible lifestyle (I do). So why not put those rose-tinted glasses on now?

Appreciate time with family, friends, or out in nature. Find ways to enjoy your work (even I managed this one). Make the most of your days off, take care of your health, and celebrate all the little victories along the way:

- Each investment we make.
- Every savings optimisation we find.
- Seeing our dividends come in.
- When our portfolio or net worth hits a milestone ($10k, $50k, $100k, etc.).

Solution #2: Actively Work on Speeding It Up

Most people focus on this one, me included. And it's hard not to. There's no shortage of ways to bring that freedom date closer. We can:

Find ways to earn more

Make sure you're being paid well for your skillset by comparing salaries and roles on sites like Indeed and Seek. You might want to take on more responsibilities, work extra hours, build additional skills, or start a second job/side hustle in your spare time, using whatever marketable skills you have. But make sure your life is still enjoyable. You'll know if you've gone too far.

Find ways to cut expenses

Probably the easiest and most fun option. Trimming expenses comes with that juicy 25x multiplier benefit we've spoken about many times. When you cut things from your life which aren't adding value, it creates that double-win of less money wasted and more cash leftover for investing. And by optimising your spending to get the same lifestyle at a lower price tag, it feels like free money!

Solution #3: Make Your Plans Come to Life

Start mapping out what your life of freedom might look like (more on this in the next chapter). Some people have concrete and detailed plans for when they no longer have to work. Others, like myself, decide to figure it out later and leave everything completely open.

For some reason, I thought I'd be happy doing nothing after retiring early. And, for a while, it was fantastic to unwind and chill out. But that doesn't last forever. You'll need some new, productive, and meaningful things to do. That's why mapping out your options is a wise move. Create a list of stuff you might like to do:

- Any skills you'd like to develop.
- Hobbies you want to work on.
- Topics you'd love to learn more about.

Can you bring some of these things into your life right now? Sometimes we put these off because they seem harder in our heads than they actually are. Of course, some things will probably have to wait until you're retired. That 6-month trip around Australia. Having lunch with your family every day. That's hard to do with a full-time work schedule.

But exploring possible part-time retirement gigs and leisurely projects? That's easy. Maybe you even try one of these ideas and love it, which could change your plans altogether. Start working on this stuff now if you can. Transitioning into your new life is much easier when you've thought about it beforehand.

Solution #4: Say "Screw It" and Semi-Retire Instead

A less obvious way to deal with the boring middle part of your FI journey is to simply retire earlier. Semi-retirement (or semi-FI) is an excellent option for the many reasons we discussed in chapter three. Now, I'll admit that there's something magical about the thought and feeling of never having to work again. But the truth is that you can get most of the benefits in less time with semi-FI.

As we covered, reaching 50% of your FI goal is the perfect benchmark for semi-retirement. Either that, or having a paid-off home, which creates a similar level of freedom by removing a large cost from your life. From here, you can start working less and living with more independence. Remember, just maintaining a small cashflow surplus which is reinvested will eventually see you reach complete FI.

Switching to part-time work and having a slightly longer overall journey will be the right move for many people. If you want to taste freedom sooner and are happy to keep working part-time, then go for it. Worst case, if you don't like semi-retirement, you can always ramp up work and savings until you can fully retire.

Clearly, there's lots we can do to sail through the boring middle part of our FI journey. Personally, I got a bit obsessive and focused mostly on Solution #2: speeding it up. Looking back now, I don't regret that choice, but I should have also spent more time considering other options.

Whichever approach you choose, remember to be eternally grateful for finding this path in the first place, and living in a country and time where this is possible. Ultimately, even just knowing you're on your way to financial independence is incredible by itself.

Goals and Rewards

We can also make the journey more enjoyable by having things to look forward to. Studies show that, counterintuitively, we often get more thrill from the anticipation of a reward than the actual reward itself. How weird is that?

So, be sure to bask in the glory of your progress. It doesn't have to have to be anything fancy or elaborate. Just take some time out to appreciate the milestones along the way, recognising where you are now, and where you started.

Take a day off and go to the beach. Head out for your favourite meal, or whatever you like. Think about how you can have little celebrations at different points of the journey to make it even sweeter and give yourself some extra motivation and encouragement to keep going. It's even cooler if you have a friend who is on the FI journey and you can celebrate each other's milestones.

As much as we plan, our lives and finances are still beholden to random events (often referred to as bad luck). So even if things aren't going as well as you'd like, cut yourself some slack and focus on the healthy actions you're taking, rather than the immediate results.

By the way, good luck can also be seen as the absence of bad luck. If nothing really bad has happened to us, we should consider ourselves fortunate. So even if we haven't won lotto, we're probably far luckier than we realise.

Sometimes there will be setbacks. That's when you should focus on process over progress. As long as you keep following the winning recipe, you'll be back on track in no time.

Building a Better Life Right Now

Sometimes we think FI will solve all our problems. It sure can solve a few. But there's plenty we can do to improve our current lives as we work towards this financial goal.

Make time for exercise

Exercise is one of the biggest contributors to positive mental and physical health. Simply being more active gives you more energy. If you can only choose 1-3 things to do outside work, make exercise one of them.

Get enough sleep

For a while, I sacrificed sleep to work more hours. This made me burnt out and grumpy. Neglecting sleep quickly catches up with you. Prioritise good quality rest and you'll feel much more productive and happier.

Consume less news

As someone who is trying to achieve something great, you'll want to minimise time spent consuming news articles and scrolling social media. These outlets are biased towards negative stories, drama, victimhood, and scary things outside your control. It's literally poison for the mind.

Enjoy nothing-time

Often we plan too many things in our spare time, leaving us stressed and overwhelmed. Give yourself space to just relax, unwind, and gather your thoughts. Do some quiet activities like reading and spending time in nature to refresh.

Be grateful

Despite what we hear, we're living in the safest and most abundant time in history. And in Australia, our living standards are already among the highest in the world. Yes, some people have it better. But more than 99% of humans who have walked the Earth have had it worse.

Live for yourself, not others

Our minds (and our lives) are often filled with things we didn't actively choose. We're led by the world around us. When we build a stricter filter for what we say yes to, our lives improve dramatically. Take control of your life, or you'll end up being pushed around like you're in a slow-motion pinball machine.

Slow down, and focus

What's the point of being so busy that we don't actually stop for a minute to take it all in? The more we do, the faster our lives go by. Now, I don't know about you, but that's not what I want. Find what activities bring you the most satisfaction in your free time and focus on those.

Congratulations on making it this far! We've now covered all the meaty parts of getting you from where you are now, to that glorious point where you're able to confidently step off the hamster wheel and do your own thing.

It's time to discuss what early retirement looks like in practice, building your new life, living off your portfolio, and other fun stuff like getting your spouse and friends on board.

This isn't the end of your journey: it's the start of your new life. Let the fun begin!

12

Your New Life of Freedom

"Every day is a bank account, and time is our currency. No one is rich, no one is poor, we've got 24 hours each." - *Christopher Rice*

In theory, once you have enough wealth to live off you can cheerfully hand in your notice at work and ride off into the sunset. And, in all honesty, that's how I thought about it.

But there's a little more to it than that. We need to sort out a few things first. Let's start with our finances, with the main question being: how do we actually live off our investments? There's a few methods for creating income from your portfolio in retirement. Here's a simple way to think about it, using the example portfolio I mentioned earlier: 50% Aussie shares / 50% international shares.

We'll assume Aussie shares provide 4% dividends and 3% capital growth (it's probably more than this when we include franking credits, but we'll be conservative). And let's say global shares return 2% dividends and 5% capital growth. When these are combined, we have a portfolio with an average return of 7% per year, made up of 3% dividends and 4% capital growth. A $1 million portfolio like this would produce around $30,000 per year in passive dividend income. The $500,000 of Aussie shares should produce $20,000 in dividends, while the $500,000 of global shares spits out $10,000 per year.

To start receiving those dividends, you'll need to turn off your automatic dividend reinvestment plan, if you haven't already. Then, to generate a total income of $40,000 (following the 4% rule), we can trim our global shares by $10,000 per year. While it feels unnatural to sell shares, it's a reasonable, sustainable, and practical thing to do because global shares are higher growth, lower income assets. We're essentially just harvesting some of the gains as the portfolio expands over time.

An alternative is to create a higher income producing portfolio, but this can dilute the benefits of diversification. That's the trade-off. And in our example, selling shares serves multiple purposes: it creates extra income to live on, *and* keeps the portfolio in line with the original 50/50 allocation.

If we don't sell anything, global shares will keep getting bigger as a percentage of the portfolio, because of the (likely) higher capital growth.

Another method to create income from a portfolio is to have all dividends reinvested automatically. Then each year just sell whatever is required to create 4% ($40,000) while keeping the portfolio in line with our chosen allocation.

While this approach may sound strange, if we reinvest our dividends then sell the same dollar-amount of shares, we're in the same position afterwards. This method can provide a little more control in keeping the exact split between funds over time.

Or, if you find the natural dividends from the portfolio is enough to live off, simply let this cash flow to your bank account and use this income for spending. And if you happen to have some investments which sustainably pay you more than 4% per year, feel free to incorporate that into your plans. 4% is a rule of thumb, not a rule of law.

Honestly, it doesn't matter too much which approach you're following. They all achieve roughly the same thing. Think about which one feels right for your situation. The most important thing is your ability to ride out any storms you might face, and just generally adapt as things change.

Markets will fluctuate a lot. There will be some great years and some painful ones. Obviously, it's better to avoid selling shares at the worst possible time, as this creates a risk of your portfolio running down.

So how do we keep our retirement chugging along smoothly when our investments are struggling? Luckily, there are plenty of ways.

Backup Plans and Flexibility Levers

Here's a few extra weapons you can have in your financial armoury:

Cash buffer

It earns little, but cash is still extremely handy to have on hand when the market and dividends take a hit. Consider keeping 5-10% (or 1-2 years spending) in an offset or savings account. If the market is down, use some cash to live on rather than selling shares. A more cautious investor may want to keep more than this, while others may be comfortable with less, and will instead focus on the other strategies mentioned here.

Flexible spending

The most underappreciated financial skill to have. Being able to temporarily reduce your spending by 10% or more during a downturn is a useful way to weather a financial storm. And it's a sensible reflex that everyone has when living through a recession, so you'll likely spend less without even realising. Ramp up your frugality and ride through the storm.

Part-time work

Another useful lever is being open to earning some part-time income. This could be done in a million different ways, either working for someone else or doing your own thing. Even one day per week at $25 per hour would pull in $10,000 a year. Double that for a couple, and increase it again for well-paid work. Think of this like a powerful income tap you can turn on and off when it suits.

Alternative income sources

You may also wish to do something like rent out a room in your house for a while to earn some extra income. Here, you could possibly generate another $10,000 per year. You can even rent out a parking space or your car these days (or sell it if you're not really using it). There are quite a few unusual income-earning opportunities when you look around.

Super

If you're retiring in your 20s, 30s or even 40s, there's a decent chance you're not even factoring super into your FI plans. This means your superannuation can be seen as the ultimate backup plan. It'll continue to grow over the years and end up being a sizable pot of additional wealth to fall back on later, should your personal investments not do as well as expected.

Pension

The last line of defence if all else fails...and I mean everything. You run your portfolio way down, you're not able or willing to work, you have no other backup plans, and you either exhaust your super or don't have any. Unless you're quite wealthy, you'll still receive a government pension which will help pay the bills. Granted, you won't be hotel-hopping around the globe, and nobody likes to think about the worst possible outcome. But in a true emergency it's worth remembering the pension is an extremely valuable safety net.

Adaptability and Strength

The more adaptable you are in the bad years, the more you can spend from your portfolio during the good years. Based on all the 'flexibility levers' I mentioned, and my preference for freedom over security, I would personally feel comfortable living off 5% of our investments each year vs the standard 4%.

But if you're a more conservative person, and you don't fancy the above strategies, you may go for an even safer withdrawal rate of 3%. Remember: this means you need a bigger portfolio, which means working longer. That's another trade-off. Whether that's worth it is up to you.

You can use a combination of the above strategies to ensure your portfolio, lifestyle, and freedom remain intact for the rest of your life. If the share market has a meltdown, maybe you spend less that year and use cash to avoid selling shares. Or, you may prefer to do some part-time work, keep your spending the same, and maybe you even earn enough so you can buy more shares while the market is down. You could also keep extra cash for that purpose if you like. It's all up to you.

Make no mistake, being able to flexibly adjust your spending and income by even just $10,000 puts you in *an incredibly strong position*. And as you become a master at managing money, following the principles you've learned in this book, that's incredibly easy.

Remember how powerful these levers are thanks to the 25x effect. Creating an extra $10,000 per year of income (or reducing spending by $10,000) is like having an extra $250,000 of investments. And if you can manage $20,000, that equates to a backup plan worth $500,000. When you apply this sort of thinking, you realise that even after leaving full-time work, you have far more control over your situation than it first appears.

Your Flex Rate and the 'Number'

The amount you can adjust your annual spending or income is called your 'flex rate'. Well, it is now because I just made up the term!

Jokes aside, this number has enormous power yet goes mostly ignored by the finance community. I've mentioned this concept several times over the years, but only recently found a nifty calculator that could confirm my suspicions with data, offering some comfort and proof for this book.

Let's say you retire with $1 million in shares and spend $40,000 per year. If you have $10,000 of flexibility in your situation, this amounts to 25% of what you need. Your flex rate is 25%.

Based on the post-FIRE calculator by Engaging Data, this 25% flex leads to a *100% long term success rate,* based over any historical time period from the last 150 years. This means your portfolio will outlast you.

Importantly, it doesn't matter when you retire (i.e., even at 20), or how long you remain retired (even 100 years!). This approach works with aggressive investment portfolios (80-100% invested in stocks), with 100% stocks producing the best long-term result.

And if you have a 40% flex rate or greater ($16,000 per year, for our example), this has safely allowed a 5% initial withdrawal rate, rather than 4%. This amount of flexibility is easier to achieve than you might think. Run through all the flexibility levers again and you'll quickly imagine several ways to create a substantial amount of flex if you need it. The higher your flex rate, the more control you have.

(You'll find an article with these examples and more on the book resources page.)

In my own situation, we could easily reduce our spending by 20%, while *almost lazily* earning part-time income equal to 80% of our expenses (we already do). This essentially gives us a flex rate of 100%, meaning that if we don't want to withdraw anything from our investments (or even spend the income), we don't have to, which practically guarantees our long term wealth.

So, when people accuse me of being overly optimistic with my assumptions or suggestions, or say that we retired with too little, I laugh. These people don't understand the sheer power you have over your situation and how to tweak the numbers to ensure success.

Let's add to this idea. At the later stages of the FI journey, people can get so focused on their 'number' that they forget to think about the bigger picture. Say your target is $1 million. You currently have $800,000.

Now, one way to look at this is "Damn it, I'm not FI yet, back to work on Monday." Another way is, "Holy shit, I'm 80% financially independent – *I can live a mostly-retired lifestyle any time I like!*"

This matters because this is not an all-or-nothing game. As I've encouraged throughout this book, we need to expand our thinking beyond yes/no, can/can't, good/bad. Most of the barriers we create are in our minds.

There's little difference between being 75%, 85%, or even 110% FI. You still have the ability and breathing space to create a fantastic life with tons of free time and all sorts of enjoyable activities, with only a small amount of income required to plug the gap (remember our chat about semi-retirement in chapter three?).

Please calculate your flex rate. It will bring you a sense of empowerment to know that your investments (while very important) are only one aspect of building and maintaining your independence.

Keep this in mind as you edge closer to your goal, so that you can start focusing more on your new life than your net worth.

Retiring with Confidence and Understanding 'Enough'

The more adaptable you're willing to be, the more secure your early retirement will be. Alternatively, the more cushion and protection you want, the longer it will take to create freedom. That's your choice.

The reality is, you aren't going to leave work and do nothing for the next 50 years. And even a small amount of personal income is a big help in ensuring your investments last forever. In fact, it's overwhelmingly likely that, later in life, your wealth grows to many times what you had when you first retired. In which case, there are countless good causes and charities for you to send that additional wealth, making your life even more meaningful.

There's no right method for everyone, so think about which backup plans feel like the best fit. These strategies will let you comfortably deal with whatever happens in your future. And because you're already wealthy upon reaching FI, it's good to remember you're in a far better position than most.

Finally, make sure you define your point of 'enough'. Too many people (even the extremely wealthy) are missing out on freedom right now, either because they want more than they need, or because they're scared of not having enough. Some have even written to me to explain their situation and ask for support.

Of course, I reply with all the important points you've read here. Sometimes it helps, other times it doesn't. For some people, there's always that nagging fear of an unknown future, and their imagination runs wild with all the things that could go wrong (while seemingly ignoring all the ways they could manage it).

If their FI goal was $1.5 million, they extend it to $2 million "just to be safe". When they hit $2 million, they worry about the markets, future health bills, unexpected expenses, helping their kids, or how their job "isn't that bad". But this addiction to 'safety' stops people from living the life they really want. And isn't that the biggest risk of all? Their minds, driven by fear, are creating reasons to stay in the known, comfortable, status quo.

Let's be real: it takes courage to break away from the rat race and claim your freedom. You must accept that the future is unknowable, yet you still need confidence in your ability to navigate whatever happens. But there's no reason to be fearful. You have *options.*

"A little bit more" is the most dangerous financial goal to have. It becomes a moving target, and a thirst we can never quench. These people are consumed, worrying about their finances and external things outside their control, when they should be turning their attention towards creating a new life and the freedom that awaits them. Let's talk about that now.

Your New Life

While working at my old job, I spent an unhealthy amount of time dreaming about being financially independent. These fantasies weren't anything elaborate. Mostly just a vision of relaxing in a comfortable chair, maybe looking at the ocean, with a peaceful smile and an internal glow of satisfaction, knowing that I was completely free to do whatever I desired for the rest of my life.

And for all the time I spent with these images, I never thought further than that. For some reason, I assumed I'd be happy living out my days taking it easy and not do much else at all.

But it doesn't really work like that. Us humans thrive on being productive. We need projects and meaningful pursuits to keep our brains ticking and our energy flowing. It sounds silly now, but I just didn't give retired life much thought. Luckily, I quickly adapted and found many enjoyable ways to spend my newfound freedom. For some people, it's easy to feel lost and directionless, not knowing how to use all the free time they now have. For this reason, you should prepare in advance for when that time comes.

How To Spend Your Freedom

"The meaning of life is to do things for their own sake." – *Naval Ravikant.*

Maybe you're smarter than me. Maybe you've already thought about all the things you'd like to do once you've reached FI. If so, fantastic! And if you haven't, that's totally okay.

How do you start planning what you'll do with your time? Here's my advice:

Firstly, think about your main motivations for pursuing FI in the first place. Are you wanting more family time? Long travel experiences? To prioritise your health? To start a passion project? Write down everything that comes to mind. This is really important. Spend time revisiting this on a regular basis to remind yourself why you're on this journey.

Next, make a list of all the things that interest you. Anything you might want to make time for. Activities you want to experience. Something you want to study or explore. People you'd like to spend more time with. Hobbies you want to take up, or get back into. Maybe a business or freelance idea you're keen to test out. Habits you want to build. Places you want to visit. Causes or charities you'd like to help.

Don't overthink it, or question whether it's practical. Just write it all down. It's probably going to be a long list, and that's okay. In fact, it's fantastic. Look at all the possibilities and things you'll soon have more time to enjoy. Remember, you don't *have* to do any of this, but it's there for inspiration. I encourage you to do this exercise as soon as possible. Not only does it give you something to work towards, but it can also give you ideas to bring into your life today.

Lifestyle Design

When we leave work, we lose a tremendous amount of structure. Our lives are built around our work, so we're forced into a structured routine. But without work, we're basically left with unlimited ways to spend our day. That can be exciting, yet also intimidating. Some people struggle with this, since it's a huge change. One solution is to create a new routine.

Start by imagining what your ideal day looks like. Remember, everyone's unique, so your ideal day will probably look different from someone else's. Maybe you're not sure what your ideal day looks like yet. To offer some insight, I'll share my personal experience. After leaving full-time work, I've noticed a similar theme from the days I enjoy the most.

These days include:

Being active. This includes a nice morning walk, some exercise or playing with the dog, and maybe a bike ride or some yard/garden work.

Being productive. For me, this usually means working on an article (or writing this book), responding to readers' comments/emails, exploring new ideas, and perhaps managing our finances.

Relaxing. I love having plenty of space during the day to gather my thoughts, ponder the universe, think about the future, and appreciate the present. Having time for reflection is so valuable, yet we largely ignore it in modern society.

Learning. Enjoying whatever book I'm reading. Or consuming a few articles, podcasts, and videos. I try to learn more about the topics I'm interested in each day. A day doesn't feel complete without this.

Enjoying nature. After moving to a greener area of Perth, we spend much more time appreciating the nature around us. Now we regularly see amazing birdlife, kangaroos in the nearby woodlands, and even long-necked turtles which come out from the lake to lay their eggs. Making this even better, we volunteer in the regional park, planting trees and helping the turtles.

Socialising. I'm an introvert by nature, so I don't need much socialising to be content. But the best days usually involve some of it. This can include catching up with friends, talking with family, or simply chatting with my partner.

Of course, there are other things I do, but you get the idea. The overall picture is a life that is far more balanced and enjoyable than my old full-time work routine. Like anyone, I'm prone to laziness and procrastination, so not everyday is a happy, productive day. But when I remember how much I enjoy these activities, it helps me refocus and use my time more wisely.

Design your lifestyle around the activities that bring you the most personal fulfilment on a daily basis.

What To Expect from Early Retirement

If you're like me, shortly after leaving work you're likely to experience or realise many of the following things:

- Each day starts when you decide it will. That alarm clock is now optional.
- No more soul-sucking commute. You can structure errands and outings to avoid traffic and busy times. I call this the 'off peak' life, and it's glorious.
- Way more time is available for anything and everything you feel like doing.
- Health gets to be a focus. You can devote extra time to exercise and preparing healthy food.
- Any work chosen from now on is completely optional.

For us, the first few months of retirement were dedicated to unwinding and decompressing from the rut of full-time work. It was about enjoying the limitless free time, considering our options (like the list from earlier) and settling into a nice, relaxed groove.

After this initial 'holiday' period, you'll find yourself feeling refreshed, with near-abundant levels of energy. All that mental and physical effort you spent at work is now freely available. Before long, you'll find yourself *wanting* to redirect this newfound energy into productive pursuits.

My partner got massively into gardening, while I started a blog. These are both activities we enjoy to this day. As time passed, I had a few more realisations:

- Working is more fun when it's something you're actually interested in. And doing it without the draining nature of a robotic, productivity-driven workplace makes it even better.
- Without direction, your mental state and happiness can suffer. This may differ between personalities, but I'm much happier working on (or learning about) things that are important to me. Don't get me wrong, I'm a laid-back guy who likes a simple life and a small to-do list, but getting stuff done feels good too.
- Time still passes relatively quickly, unless you literally do nothing. But that's not a great idea either (see my previous point). It seems inevitable that a good life is going to feel like it goes fast, because you'll be busy doing stuff you enjoy. Maybe that's the trade-off.
- Money is less meaningful after reaching Financial Independence. It still matters, sure. But mostly, money is a bunch of numbers on a screen or a spreadsheet. I've already said FI is more about life than money. But this fully sinks in after you leave the rat race.

Your new mission (and the real lesson here) is to find engaging and productive activities that you'd do for free. Because if you're just doing it for the money, then it can't be that good.

Create a life where you're doing things which are good for their own sake. Looking after yourself, nurturing relationships, being creative, helping others, using your skills, and so on. These things don't require a financial reward to be worthwhile.

While some of my realisations are to be expected, there's also some things about retirement you might find unusual.

Early Retirement Surprises

Freedom can be scary

Looking at a lifetime of freedom ahead of you is like winning the lottery. At first, you can't believe your luck. But then your mind may become flooded with options, ideas, and opportunities. Now you start feeling a little overwhelmed. You have too many choices! Sure, it's a high-quality problem, but it's still a problem nonetheless.

Having complete freedom can be daunting. Because of this unique opportunity, you might start feeling like you must do something ultra-meaningful in a save-the-whole-world type of way. But then you realise that just doing things that mean something to you is good enough. If you're being productive in your own way, you'll derive a sense of meaning from that. You can then relax into your new life and carry on at your own pace. Another reminder of why it's good to have a list of ideas ready beforehand.

You forget that you're retired

After a while, you'll be going about your day, maybe out for a mid-morning walk, working on a project, reading a book, and it hits you! You remember that everything you do is optional because you're FI. Alternatively, maybe you're in a bad mood for whatever reason (yes, you still experience the full range of emotions!), and then you remember that you're more fortunate than almost everyone on the entire planet. These little sledgehammers to the forehead often catch me by surprise and remind me to be grateful.

Loneliness is a possibility

In contrast to the previous point, you also find yourself acutely aware that you have way more time than everyone else. This means, sadly, it can still be tricky to organise catch ups with friends and family. In this way, you aren't 'in sync' with most of the population, which has its own pros and cons.

Introverts (like myself) are more than happy doing their own thing most of the time, so this probably won't be an issue. But extroverts who thrive on interaction will need to make sure their weeks are filled with other social activities. Whether it's through volunteering, part-time work, or making friends while out walking or at your daytime gym sessions, it's vital that you create a lifestyle that meets all your specific needs. Like my partner, you may realise you miss the social aspect of working and decide to go back part-time.

Mindset and Outlook

As time goes on, you may also find your attitude changes in a few different ways. Firstly, because you've stepped off the glorified hamster-wheel, you'll care even less what others think of you. This doesn't mean you stop showering, but maybe you'll find it easier to make decisions and think more clearly. Besides, if you ever need reminding of your good judgement, simply look at your level of freedom compared to most people your age.

Essentially, your life will be more independent than ever. You'll be living in a calmer, more peaceful world. Almost like you're in some parallel universe. You'll have time to literally smell the roses, look at the clouds, and appreciate each day and the freedom you have. You'll know that any work taken must be enjoyable, and can be dropped or modified when it no longer suits you. The satisfaction and comfort this brings is a game-changer.

Because of these reasons, your health and wellbeing will typically improve as well. You'll have better sleep. Less stress. Improved nutrition. More movement. And a more balanced, happier lifestyle. All these things are so much easier once you control your time.

Explaining your Situation

Financial independence enables you to live differently from most people. That can make for some awkward conversations.

I've had people reach out to me who can afford to leave work, but they have concerns about what to tell people and what others will think of them.

After all, retiring extremely early is so out of the realm of 'normal' that coming straight out with it is like opening a can of worms. Let's tackle these tricky issues.

"What Do I Tell People at Work?"

You have a few options. Personally, I just told people the real story at the end. A few already knew what I was doing, but most didn't. I'm sure they thought it was strange and many probably assumed I was full of shit. But there were no problems, and management left me with: "If you want to come back, you're welcome to."

The real decision is whether to make up a story or just have those potentially awkward conversations. Neither of which is a big deal in the grand scheme of things. Besides, what can your workplace or workmates do or say at this point that would be an issue? You don't need employment any more.

Here are some ideas on what to say:

1. Say you're taking a long break and plan to live off your savings.

2. Say you're just having some time off before eventually starting something new.

3. Tell the truth: that you have enough savings and investments to support you and no longer need to work.

Don't feel guilty. You've earned the right to do whatever the hell you like. Taking time off and going into cruise mode for a while is perfectly fine.

What to Say When Someone Asks "So, What Do You Do?"

This can be the pinnacle of awkward conversations. You'll probably need to test a few different answers to see what works for you. I've been getting away with saying, "Oh, I just do some writing part-time."

Initially, you can use, "I'm taking some time off at the moment." Then, later, once you get around to starting new activities, you can use my approach and say, "I just do X part-time." If they ask how you manage that, you can simply say, "We have some savings and/or investments and don't spend a lot, so we manage okay without working full-time."

This avoids sounding like you're saying, "I'm rich," which unfortunately is what people might interpret if you brag about being financially independent. This way, they're more likely to think you're just a regular person with some savings.

Obviously, if you're feeling energetic, you can open that can of worms and explain the whole situation. Regardless, some people will still think certain things about you for being different. In that case, let them be the ones who feel uncomfortable.

Now, it's also worth seeing how you can get people close to you along for the ride, starting with your friends.

Getting Your Friends on Board

Chatting about finances with your friends is sometimes easier than with a spouse, given your lives and choices are independent of one other. So, reach out to friends who may be interested in building a brighter future, and share with them what you're up to. Not in a preachy way, but more like: "Hey, here's what I've been learning, I can help you get started if you're interested."

You can gently nudge them in the right direction with things like "Man, I got a great deal on my mortgage/internet/whatever, recently." Or casually check your phone and be like, "Oh wow, I got a dividend today... the coffee's on me!" They'll probably say, "What, how does that work?" And voila, you have a good shot at hooking them into your universe.

Having a buddy along for the ride is valuable, so that you can share ideas, wins, and progress together. But not everyone will bite (most people won't!). They're too accustomed to their current lifestyle and way of thinking, and not interested in change.

If your circle of friends isn't keen, you can reach out to new people and even connect with others in online forums and groups. You'd be surprised at how many people in your state (even nearby) are interested in this stuff. I have a few suggested groups on the book resources page.

Now, the bigger and potentially more difficult task...

How to Get Your Spouse on Board

What happens when you're totally motivated by financial freedom, but your spouse isn't? Maybe they don't see the appeal of retiring early, or would rather 'live for today', buying a regular stream of treats and luxuries with their pay check.

We can't brush this off. It's important for the relationship that you work together. A couple in an endless game of tug-of-war to see who can extract the most is not a healthy situation. I won't lie, this may be tricky. There are emotions, deeply held beliefs, and core values at play. First, let's start with what NOT to do.

Don't constantly nag your partner to do something. Don't wear them down with criticisms. It won't work. In fact, it's likely to backfire and they'll dig their heels in deeper and resent you for it. Your spouse might feel like you're trying to control their every move or preventing them from doing certain things.

It's easy to say, "Well, I don't do that to my partner." But I think most of us have been guilty of this in some way. No couple agrees on every aspect of their lives, financial or otherwise.

We can't force others to think and believe what we do (though the fantasy remains!). But we may be able to influence them in various ways, and that's where our energy should go.

Lead by Example

Often, the disconnect comes when two people have different spending desires. The low spender thinks, "Why can't they be happy with less?" Some people genuinely worry that spending less will make them miserable, so this is a tough one.

How can you get your spouse to see it's possible to live well without spending everything you earn? Show them. With everything you do. The activities and hobbies you pursue. How you spend your time. And the way you approach life. Rather than preaching, become an undeniable example.

You can also do this with your peer group and even in the community. When we see others enjoying a picnic, biking around town, hearing about their future freedom plans or the simple hobbies they're so passionate about, we think to ourselves, "That actually seems pretty good."

This is why the FIRE movement has grown so much in recent years. We see people like us who are on this path, or already free, and realise, "Damn, why aren't I doing that?" Sometimes, it just takes a few examples for our brains to believe something is achievable.

Paint a Picture

Inspire your spouse by showing them how fantastic life could be if you follow this path. The details will be different for everyone, but the benefits are the same.

Think of how to get them excited with all the things they could do without a full-time work schedule and bills getting in the way. Show them that the greatest luxury of all is having time to do whatever they like. Take a few days off together in the middle of the week – not to go holidaying anywhere, but just to get some appreciation for how luxurious an ordinary day can be when you're not burdened by work.

Figure out what will most inspire them. Maybe it's the ability to be fully immersed in your kids' lives while they're young. It could be enjoying more time together as a couple, going to the beach when everyone's at work, starting your own little work-from-home businesses while you take breaks together, or heading on week-long trips at a moment's notice.

A discussion around the future and what you could achieve as a couple is often all it takes to encourage healthier long-term thinking.

Paint a Different Picture

If the 'inspiring future' didn't generate any excitement, discuss what happens if you *don't* do it. What if we don't bother saving? What if we focus on today, and disregard the future? How does that generally work out?

We don't have to look far to see why this is a terrible approach to personal finance and life in general. Financial insecurity is a huge cause of stress, unhappiness, and divorce. Health issues, unemployment, or dissatisfaction in career and life direction creates huge anxiety and hopelessness for anyone who is in poor financial shape.

Why would you voluntarily put yourself in this position? 'Living for today' is a beautifully simple philosophy to have. The problem is that in the modern world we interpret this to mean spending as much as possible.

But taken to its end point, it's also dangerous, childish, and even immoral (since we expect others – typically the government – to save us when something goes wrong). At this point, saving and investing for the future makes sense. If your spouse hasn't stormed off by now, they may begin to see things differently.

What If They're a Full-Blown Consumer?

Well, this will be a mighty challenge. Frankly, I don't like your chances. Spending and consumption is a religion for some people. Questioning this religion usually makes people very angry, since their whole identity revolves around it. At this point, you could explain how we already have the highest living standards in history, and reside in one of the wealthiest countries in the world. This sole point highlights just how strange it is to still want more. To shrug that off because it doesn't *feel* like we're rich, relative to a small handful of other ultra-rich humans, is simply insane. This is the highest form of entitlement. It shows a lack of gratitude, humility, and perspective.

Look, it's entirely possible that your partner just doesn't have the same 'bullshit detector' as you. Most spending desires come from the billions spent on advertising, which is carefully designed to make us feel inadequate, so that companies can sell us stuff that will (supposedly) make us feel better, richer, sexier, happier, healthier, more respected, and more admired.

After all, people aren't really buying products, they're buying feelings.

See Their Side

Both parties need to feel heard and understood, so you want to see where your spouse is coming from. If they have no interest in financial independence, try to find out more.

What are their priorities? Do they have other goals in mind? Do they really love their job?

Achieving a happy middle-ground is often a great outcome. For example, if you want to save 60% of your income and your spouse wants to save nothing, maybe you can agree to 30%.

After a while, your spouse will probably notice that they're just as happy as before. They may even become excited when they watch these savings grow through your investments. Some people dismiss the idea of building wealth precisely because they don't think it's possible for them. Attitudes can change quickly once we believe we can do something.

You Could Separate Your Finances

This approach may sound unusual, but it can work. Each spouse pays their share of the household bills, and aside from that, their income is free to spend as they please. Alternatively, you could also set up an agreed spending allowance for each person. This helps the non-FI spouse see that they can still enjoy things they're accustomed to. And remember, if your spouse has no interest in financial independence, it doesn't mean you can't shoot for it. Any personal savings you can put towards investments creates less reliance on work with every passing year.

This lets the FI-focused spouse use their money to create freedom, while the higher-spending spouse gets to keep their current lifestyle as is.

The Boardroom Approach

With this strategy, each partner gets to approve or reject the spending decisions of the other person for purchases over an agreed amount (like $20 or $50).

If your proposed purchases fill a genuine need, your spouse will recognise this and give you the green-light. Well, provided you have a healthy relationship!

Even though this approach sounds like the epitome of teamwork, in reality most couples won't enjoy it because of how it limits their personal freedom. This is unfortunate because this method is arguably the most open, honest, and transparent of all. It fosters conversations about spending and values, and helps the couple become a real team with better communication, understanding and accountability.

Remember, a couple is effectively in the business of life together. Each decision made either helps or hinders this 'business' from achieving its goals – whether it's buying a house or saving for retirement.

What Worked for Me

Luckily, my partner was on board with the idea of retiring early to begin with. The 'spending less' bit was more of a challenge, but to her credit, she was willing to test it. All up, it was a combination of painting a compelling picture of the future, discussing what was important to each of us, making plans together, and then taking steps forward.

Over time, our spending consistently fell as we improved our habits and focused on investing as much as possible. We were left with the realisation that this didn't cost us any happiness. In fact, we were continually surprised at how easy it was to string together lots of small changes, which created a big benefit. These chunks of progress provided motivation for further improvements, and the life-enhancing snowball continued to grow.

I'm under no illusions that there's an easy answer to getting your spouse on the same page. So open up the communication lines, find out what values and beliefs motivate your spouse, and create a plan that works for you both. Hopefully, they will see that all this FIRE stuff isn't about reusing toilet paper, eating roadkill, and living under a bridge to avoid work. It's about having options and experiencing a more meaningful life.

Sometimes the best way to help your spouse or friend is to simply point them to the resources which have helped you. You could give them links to the websites or videos that you learned from. Maybe you even hand them this book. Lessons are often more readily received from an authoritative-seeming stranger than those closest to us.

We covered a lot of important stuff in this chapter. Now, as we come towards the end, I'd like to offer a few take-home messages, parting inspiration, and some final pieces of advice.

13

Final Thoughts

"In the truest sense, freedom cannot be bestowed; it must be achieved." - *Franklin D. Roosevelt*

As we wrap up, I'd like to offer some final thoughts to motivate you to act on what we've been talking about. I'll truly consider this book a success if it inspires you to start building a brighter future by working towards financial independence.

Of course, I know that changes can be tricky, and the easy option is to stick with the status quo. To remind you why taking this path is so important, let's consider the alternative outcome.

If you don't take action despite having new information, it often leads to regret. Research has been done on the biggest regrets of the elderly and dying people. Overwhelmingly, most of the answers are based around the following themes (and notice the link between these regrets and the benefits of FI):

"I wish I hadn't worked so much."

We spend most of our lives working to earn money, so that we can spend this on things, come home exhausted, and zone out on technology before it's time for bed. Then we get up and do it all over again.

From a very young age, we went to school, maybe to university, and then we started work. When have you experienced true freedom? Basically never. Meaningful work is an important part of life, but it shouldn't *be* your life.

"I wish I'd had the courage to live a life true to myself and care less about what others think."

We worry about what people will think of us if we don't live a certain way or buy the same things that others have. Develop the courage to pursue what matters to you, and to ignore what doesn't. Even if everyone is pushing you in a certain direction, it's your life, not theirs.

Start paving your own way in the world and forget the opinion of others. The most important opinion is your own. In the long run, what other people think or say about us fades away, and you're left with either a life you're happy about, or wishing you had done something different.

"I wish I spent more time with family and friends."

Our current lifestyles make it harder to maintain and experience good relationships.

A level of financial independence lets you spend less time working and more time with your kids, catching up with friends, visiting family, playing with your pets, and living an all-round more balanced, enjoyable lifestyle.

Just because everyone else is 'busy' doesn't mean we should accept our jam-packed schedules as an acceptable way to live.

"I wish I'd let myself be happier."

People often take life so seriously, when we should really see it as a big adventure.

We're working hard to get somewhere, but we never really 'arrive'. We're worried about trying new things, changing direction, or taking the road less travelled. This also feeds into our fear of what others will think.

With more freedom, life is happier and less stressful. You can be present in what you're doing, because you're not trying to fit so many things into a limited amount of free time.

And when life is no longer about status, climbing the ladder, or staying afloat, you can enjoy each day, relax, and stop being so damn serious.

The fundamental truth: nobody wishes they worked more. Everybody wishes they had more time.

You have a unique opportunity to build a very different life. The life you really want. Not the default option that most people end up with.

The one thing I've heard repeatedly from readers, regardless of age, is that they wish they knew about this earlier and started sooner. We all have feelings like that. In fact, there are several things I'd like to tell younger Dave about work, life, and money.

Work

Change Happens

Your first job won't be your last, so it doesn't have to be perfect. Your interests and motivations will shift over time, leading you in new directions. Many (if not most) people end up doing work they never imagined as a fresh-faced teenager leaving school.

That's the way it should be. As time goes on, you'll grow as a person and figure out what you really like and don't like, in terms of job roles and work environments. Indoors vs outdoors? Noisy vs quiet? Large team vs solo? High pressure vs low pressure? Variation vs repetition? Creative vs technical? You get the idea.

Forget about having it all figured out straight away – nobody does! Work and life is a giant game of trial and error. Over time, you'll get better at it and closer to doing something you love.

It's stressful to think about what you're going to do for the next 60 years. Just take it one step at a time. Besides, if you're good with money, work will be optional before too long (say, 10-20 years). And that takes the pressure off, allowing you to choose work for satisfaction, instead of a pay check.

Your Interests

Aim for an industry that you're genuinely interested in, not just one that pays well. The key is finding something which suits your personality, in an area that intrigues you. Maybe you're a people person and love communication and deal-making. Perhaps you're quiet and prefer working with numbers and data. Either way, you'll struggle if your job role doesn't match your personality.

Also, if you're doing a job solely for the money, you won't be satisfied for long. The lure of more money quickly fades when you dread getting up in the morning. One of your main missions in life is to find work you enjoy for its own sake.

Find a way to use your skills and abilities to help others. You don't have to be the smartest person. You just have to be passionate and keep learning. What are you good at that other people struggle with? What do you love that others find boring? What would feel worthwhile even if you didn't get paid for it? In answering these questions, you'll find some good hints at what your ideal work may be.

Earning Potential

If you can get into a job or industry that pays well, and the work sounds okay (but not fantastic), consider diving in for a few years to get cashed up. You'll be able to build your 'freedom fund' faster this way, but you may enjoy the journey less. If you do it right, you could have a mortgage-free home or be able to semi-retire within 5-7 years.

Chasing higher income can be appealing when you're unsure about what work you want to do. I had no clue I'd be so passionate about personal finance and investing until my early 20s, let alone writing, which came much later. There's no right or wrong approach. Follow your interests, but if there's an opportunity to make good money doing something different, consider that too.

Life

Decisions and Direction

Take 100% responsibility for your life and the choices you make. Don't make excuses. Every excuse makes you mentally and emotionally weaker. Life may throw shitty things your way, but it's your job to deal with those challenges and move on.

Don't blame anyone else for your situation. Playing a victim leaves you powerless. It feels like there's no point doing anything because life just 'happens' to you. But when you take responsibility, you regain control and ownership of your life. That's powerful. There are countless stories of people in worse situations than you who turned their lives around, if you need more motivation or self-belief. And don't be too self-congratulatory when you succeed, either. Luck plays a role, both good and bad.

Be sure to map your own path in life. After all, doing the same thing as the crowd gets the same result. You're reading this book because you know there must be a better way. *Decide* how you want your life to be, rather than letting life decide for you. It doesn't have to be precise: just imagine your ideal future and work towards making that a reality.

Health and Relationships

I'd also tell Younger Dave that your health is far more important than you recognise right now. Without it, you literally have nothing. Look after yourself. Exercise regularly. Don't drink too much. Find healthy meals and snacks you enjoy and eat mostly these. You'll feel much better for it.

The worse you eat, the more lethargic you are, making you less likely to exercise, creating a downward spiral. Learning to make simple food and take care of yourself is a valuable life skill that will serve you well. Find time for quiet reflection, quality sleep, and spending time outside in nature. This keeps your mind in a peaceful state and helps you focus on your big goals rather than getting bogged down in the day-to-day details.

Look for others who are like-minded to hang out with and learn from. Spend time with positive people who think differently from the masses. People who have ideas and take action. Not those who complain and point fingers. You'll naturally find yourself drawn to those with similar values to yourself. And, lastly, when it comes to friends, quality beats quantity.

Confidence and Self-worth

What matters is not what others think of you, but what you think of you. Make sure your self-esteem doesn't rely on outside validation. You'll see plenty of people competing for popularity on social media by manufacturing a perfect looking life. Ignore this.

Often this is done for attention and acceptance. But this unhealthy ego-boost becomes an addiction that people can't live without, which is a recipe for depression. You can't control what others feel or say about you, so your self-worth needs to be built on who you are as a person.

What are your good qualities? Are you kind? Are you helpful? Do you have empathy and respect for others? What can you do with your life that you can be proud of? These things build a reservoir of confidence that you can carry with you, no matter what anyone else thinks or says.

Money

Saving Matters

Money is a tool, not a toy. It has the power to change your life, for good or for bad. Once you build a healthy respect for money, you'll never have to worry about it because there will be an ever-growing surplus that exceeds your needs.

Managing money is one of the most underappreciated skills on earth. It affects everyone, yet most people are awful at it. We can use money to create freedom and abundance, through saving and investing. But we can also use it to create slavery and stress, through bad habits, debt, and expensive tastes.

As soon as you start earning, save a good chunk of your income. Use this for a cash cushion, buying a home, or investing. If you're not saving, fix your spending before you chase more money. There's no amount of income you can't spend.

Wants vs Needs

Learn the difference. Be honest with yourself. If you do, you'll be wealthier than most, in dollar terms and in life satisfaction. You'll realise that most of our expenses are completely optional, and not necessary for a happy life.

By living in the rich modern world, you've already hit the jackpot. The ultra-wealthy of 100 years ago couldn't even imagine how the average person lives today – the entertainment, technology, conveniences, healthcare, all of it.

Facing this truth helps you feel grateful for the life you have, while working towards the future you want, which is all about being free to pursue what interests you, not having to stress about anything, and having total control of your time.

Long-term Thinking

One thing that will help you master money is the ability to think long term. This is also known as delayed gratification. Developing the ability to forgo something today for larger benefits later is crucial. Learning about compound interest is the best way to realise the importance of thinking long-term.

Investing $10,000, with an annual return of 7%, becomes around $300,000 in 50 years. That's a single investment with nothing extra added. Any amount of money, invested wisely, can multiply itself repeatedly, forever. When you see what your savings could turn into, this reinforces the importance of not wasting money.

Investing

Don't assume a complex or exciting investment strategy will work better than a simple one. The opposite is usually true. Boring investing is profitable investing. And since most of your wealth in the first 10-15 years will come from saving rather than investment performance, there's no need to chase high returns.

The goal is passive income and growing wealth from your investments. Choose a strategy that is easy, reliable, and requires little effort. There's no extra points (or returns) for making it harder than necessary. Your time and energy is valuable and better spent elsewhere.

A Quick Reminder...

Here's a brief summary of why we pursue financial independence:

- Get our lives and our freedom back, gaining complete control of our time.
- Work as much or as little as we like, choosing work based on personal satisfaction, without financial pressure.
- Devote more time to our health and wellbeing, making sure we're taking care of ourselves physically and mentally.
- Give our relationships the time and attention they deserve.
- Live at a more leisurely pace, so we can enjoy each day rather than rushing around, stressed out.
- Choose exactly what's worth spending our time on. This powerful filter is like a superpower that nobody else has.

Ultimately, financial independence gives us freedom and options. And this process starts as soon as we begin the journey and build some savings.

Whether you just want to reduce work to be a more active parent, pursue your hobbies, care for a loved one, or start a small business (knowing your personal bills are already paid for), building wealth amplifies your ability to do almost anything in life.

On a Personal Note

Deciding at a young age to get serious about my finances is the best thing I've ever done.

As Mr Money Mustache once wrote in his article, *A Millionaire is Made Ten Bucks At A Time*: "If you start respecting your tens in your 20s, you'll be retired by your 30s."

There aren't many things that change your life. But financial independence can.

For me, it's about being able to move through life at my own pace and having the freedom to pursue things that I find interesting. There's more space to think about life, my place in the world, and the direction I'm heading.

I love the simple things: like being able to meet a friend for a mid-morning coffee during the week, go for long walks with my partner anytime of the day, and play with our dog until he's exhausted.

I found a new passion in writing, something I'd never done or even considered before in my life. I've made new friends and found likeminded people who share the same values, some of whom have also retired early!

As I mentioned earlier, we took the opportunity to move to a different area of Perth, with abundant nature, more open space, and less traffic. Back then, we weren't familiar with this location, so we did a drive-by to look at a rental house opposite the regional park.

As we drove along, open parkland to my left, I was gobsmacked to see a long-necked turtle walking across the grass. I couldn't believe what I was seeing. We stopped and watched from a distance.

"Oh my god, no way!" I said.

There was nobody around. Just this huge open space, us, and this turtle.

The turtle sat under a tree and began digging a hole.

"It must be laying its eggs!"

"This is amazing, we *have to* move here."

We rented that house for more than four years, and recently bought a house on the same street. We now do local volunteering, planting trees and helping these beautiful creatures cross the road during laying season. Each spring, the mother turtles come out to lay their eggs, with several doing so in our garden! We liaise with volunteer groups and turtle experts, protect nests from predators like ravens and foxes, and about six months later, tiny hatchlings emerge – their shells the size of a 20-cent coin.

In fact, I'm taking breaks in between writing this book to take these baby turtles across to the lake. Every single one mesmerizes me.

The hatchlings like to warm up in the sun. They stretch their legs, and finally, when the coast is clear, they make a dash for the water – swimming off into an enormous lake. To them, it must be a giant, unknown world. But they don't worry, or procrastinate. They just go.

I sit there for ages, in awe of the whole situation. At that moment, I feel there is nothing else I would rather be doing. "How incredible is this?" I think.

All I can hear are birds calling, water splashing, and trees rustling in the gentle breeze. All I can feel is peace and gratitude. I wonder why I so deeply enjoy this experience. I realise: these turtles are now free. Free to enjoy their world and everything in it, at their own pace.

It's such a privilege to do things like this, which, interestingly, almost no other locals realise I'm doing because they're always at work! These moments are yet another, 'Holy shit, this is amazing!' sledgehammer to the face. I had no idea what would happen after quitting my job. But this story shows the beautiful way life can evolve when you are no longer tied to a busy full-time work schedule.

Freedom creates a more enriching life in ways that are hard to imagine.

Parting Words

We've covered a lot of ground in this book. You'll notice a good portion of my writing is around mindset and philosophy. That's because having the right outlook drives everything. It helps us find solutions to problems. Opportunities instead of hurdles. Reasons to be grateful rather than resentful. And the confidence to do something different, rather than accept the standard route.

What I've shared is not the only way to become financially independent. Hell, it may not even be the best way. There are plenty of people out there smarter than I am. But this should also tell you something: you don't need to be highly educated, earn a huge income, or devise a genius strategy to change your life and reach your financial goals.

Pursuing financial independence is straightforward, but that doesn't mean it's easy. We need to earn our achievements in life. Like an athlete who wants to win a gold medal, we can't have the benefits without putting in time, effort, and dedication.

In modern day Australia (and other rich countries), we have an incredible opportunity to use our income to create astounding freedom and build a happier, more satisfying existence.

That's what it's all about. Not avoiding work or accumulating money for the sake of it. But building a meaningful life that excites us, and making the most of our limited time on this planet.

We start by zooming out and recognising how much our lifestyles and spending habits have changed over time, thanks to our increasing prosperity created by the global economy, innovation, and human endeavour. As you now know, that's why this massive opportunity exists where it didn't before.

From income, we create savings. From savings, we create investments.

From investments, we create wealth. From wealth, we create freedom.

The key is building a life you enjoy which enables you to save a good chunk of your pay. To do that, find a money management style that works for you. Maybe it's a budget, bucketing, or (my personal favourite) the habit of questioning everything.

Build an emergency fund as you start working on the biggest costs in your life. Optimising the big stuff goes a long way towards increasing your savings rate. Then, move onto the smaller stuff, which can still be deceivingly expensive. And remember that all of this is flexible. You can spend more on what matters to you most if you work hard on cutting what doesn't. If you're happy with the trade-off, go for it.

Once your spending is optimised, look for ways to increase your income to grow your investments faster. Maybe it's overtime, finding a better job, levelling up, or even starting an enjoyable side-gig.

Practice building a more stoic and abundant mindset, helping you deal with setbacks and frustrations, while looking for solutions and ways to be proactive. Keep yourself physically and mentally healthy. Wealth is pointless if you're stressed and miserable.

Build your investments one purchase at a time. Invest regularly, as much as you can, into a simple, low-cost, diversified share portfolio. Index funds are an excellent choice for hassle-free lifelong investing. Along the way, your growing wealth provides increasing income and freedom. You can wait until you've reached FI, step off early to move into semi-retirement, or simply take big breaks along the way.

When the markets get rough, flick back to chapter ten to cement those key investing principles into your mind. This will help you stay the course and focus on the big picture. Be a laid-back long-term owner, not a twitchy short-term trader.

Give yourself mini-goals and milestones along the way. Celebrate your progress. Our brains love the anticipation of rewards, so find ways to keep yourself motivated. Even if that means spending a little more, if you enjoy the journey, it's worthwhile.

Take a moment to think about what your new life might look like. What do you want to do with all this freedom? It's important that we're working towards something, not just trying to escape work.

Create a genuinely balanced lifestyle that's filled with activities you enjoy, where you can become a healthier, happier version of yourself. From your wealthy position, you can do something more meaningful, or contribute to the world in a positive way.

When you decide that financial independence is something you really want, commit to it. Your thoughts and actions will naturally start aligning with your goal, making it easier than you expect.

The truth is, you create your own outcome. You can follow the standard approach and strap in for 40 years on a glorified hamster wheel. Or you can do something different.

Everyone's personal circumstances and journeys are unique, so take this information and adapt it to your own situation. This book isn't a list of rules. More like a list of principles, lessons, and ideas.

At first, the idea of working for only a decade or so to create a lifetime of freedom sounds insane. But I trust you can now see that financial independence is not only possible, but achievable.

I hope you're inspired to take action and start working towards a more exciting future. I wish you all the best on your own journey. Thank you for reading.

-Dave

Afterword

I appreciate you taking the time to read this book. I truly hope it has brought you value. Here's a few more things you might like to check out.

My Website: strongmoneyaustralia.com

Here you'll find a library of content on all sorts of topics related to financial independence. Sign up to my newsletter to get my latest thoughts and see what I'm working on.

Book Resources: strongmoneyaustralia.com/bookextras

Get links to all the content I mentioned throughout this book, plus additional tools, resources, and action steps to help you get started.

Did you enjoy this book?

It would mean a lot if you could leave a quick review on Amazon. Even just a line or two is great. This helps other readers discover the book and spreads the message of financial independence even further. Thanks!

References

Chapter 2: Our Opportunity for Freedom

1. Loaf of bread cost 10x less in 1975 - https://mccrindle.com.au/article/blog/40-years-of-change-1975-to-today/
2. US household spending study - https://www.theatlantic.com/business/archive/2012/04/how-america-spends-money-100-years-in-the-life-of-the-family-budget/255475/
3. Australian wages in 1966 - https://www.ausstats.abs.gov.au/ausstats/free.nsf/0/199FD6E4B83FFEC1CA2575160011AA66/$File/63020_SEP1967.pdf
4. Australian wages in 2016 - https://www.abs.gov.au/AUSSTATS/abs@.nsf/Lookup/6302.0Main+Features1May%202016?OpenDocument=
5. Wages growth since 1900 - https://stanfordbrown.com.au/wp-content/uploads/2021/10/SB-Monthly-Investment-Markets-Report-5-Oct-2021.pdf
6. Average full-time wage in 2021 - https://www.abs.gov.au/statistics/labour/earnings-and-working-conditions/average-weekly-earnings-australia/may-2021
7. Median full-time wage in 2021 - https://www.abs.gov.au/statistics/labour/earnings-and-work-hours/characteristics-employment-australia/aug-2021/
8. RBA Paper on inflation and the cost of living - https://www.rba.gov.au/publications/bulletin/2014/mar/pdf/bu-0314-4.pdf
9. Australia's wealthy citizens: high median wealth per capita - https://www.news.com.au/finance/money/wealth/australian-adults-wealthie

st-in-the-world-new-global-report-finds/news-story/8fffdc6a918 5064a153dde4f57e0b508

10. Advertising smoking to women - https://en.wikipedia.org/wiki/Torch es_of_Freedom

Chapter 3: The Fundamentals of Financial Independence

1. Credit Suisse Yearbook on long term equity market returns, including Australia - https://www.credit-suisse.com/media/assets/corporate/docs/about-us/research/publications/credit-suisse-global-investment-returns-yearbook-2021-summary-edition.pdf

2. Long term total returns of Australia, US & UK - https://www.rba.gov.au/speeches/2018/sp-so-2018-12-13.html

3. Australian equity market over the last 100 years - https://www.rba.gov.au/publications/bulletin/2019/jun/the-australian-equity-market-over-the-past-century.html

4. Real returns on Australian shares since 1900 - https://www.firstlinks.com.au/wins-australian-versus-us-investors-local-shares

5. Trinity Study calculations and explanation - https://engaging-data.com/visualizing-4-rule/

6. Compound interest calculator - https://www.moneygeek.com/compound-interest-calculator/

7. Median hourly pay rate in 2022 - https://www.abs.gov.au/statistics/labour/earnings-and-working-conditions/employee-earnings/aug-2021

Chapter 5: Big Wins to Supercharge Your Savings Rate

1. 77% of Aussie homes have at least one spare bedroom - https://www.abs.gov.au/statistics/people/housing/housing-occupancy-and-costs/2019-20
2. Australian homes the biggest in the world, with fewer people living in them - https://theconversation.com/size-does-matter-australias-addiction-to-big-houses-is-blowing-the-energy-budget-70271

Chapter 6: Next Level Optimisation

1. Government childcare subsidy - https://www.servicesaustralia.gov.au/your-income-can-affect-child-care-subsidy?context=41186
2. World land use - https://ourworldindata.org/land-use

Chapter 7: Income, Skills, and Mindset

1. Average rental value of spare rooms - https://flatmates.com.au/info/australia-s-most-valuable-spare-rooms
2. Minimum wage history - https://en.wikipedia.org/wiki/Minimum_wage_law
3. Inflation calculator - https://www.rba.gov.au/calculator/annualDecimal.html

Chapter 8: Property vs Shares for Financial Independence

1. Percentage of positive return years for Australian shares - https://files .marketindex.com.au/files/statistics/historical-returns-infographic-2019-updated.pdf
2. ASX returns for ten-year periods - https://www.vanguard.com.au/personal/learn/smart-investing/markets-and-economy/why-the-asx-will-continue-to-rise

Chapter 9: Simplified Share Investing

1. 20% of stocks responsible for entire market return - https://awealthofcommonsense.com/2016/05/the-sp-500-is-the-worlds-largest-momentum-strategy/
2. Vanguard paper on home bias and asset allocation - https://www.vanguard.ca/documents/home-bias-allocation.pdf

Chapter 10: Investment Principles for Long Term Success

1. Long term total returns of Australia, US & UK - https://www.rba.gov.au/speeches/2018/sp-so-2018-12-13.html
2. S&P 500 total return calculator - https://dqydj.com/sp-500-return-calculator/

Chapter 11: Super, Mortgages, and Enjoying the Journey

1. The safest and most abundant time in history: *Enlightenment Now* by Stephen Pinker - https://stevenpinker.com/publications/enlightenment-now-case-reason-science-humanism-and-progress

Chapter 12: Your New Life of Freedom

1. Top Regrets of the Dying - https://bronnieware.com/blog/regrets-of-the-dying/

About the Author

After becoming financially independent at 28, Dave Gow started blogging to share his experience and help others create more freedom in their lives. He lives in Perth with his partner and their bulldog.

You can connect with me on:
- https://strongmoneyaustralia.com
- https://twitter.com/strongmoneyaus
- https://www.facebook.com/StrongMoneyAustralia

www.ingramcontent.com/pod-product-compliance
Lightning Source LLC
Chambersburg PA
CBHW071546210326
41597CB00019B/3141